GROW TO LOVE

GROW TO LOVE

Developing caring relationships:

A resource book for groups

JEAN C. GRIGOR

THE SAINT ANDREW PRESS
EDINBURGH

First published in 1977 by
THE SAINT ANDREW PRESS
121 George Street, Edinburgh.

This new and completely revised
edition published in 1980
Copyright © Jean C. Grigor, 1980

ISBN 0 7152 0437 8

Printed in Great Britain by
Robert MacLehose and Co. Ltd.
Printers to the University of Glasgow

CONTENTS

FOREWORD

Christian groups are legion. Some just happen among the members of a congregation because individuals feel the impulse to meet one another at a deeper level than is usually possible in many Church activities. Others are planned as part of the pastoral policy. Many would see in this development, in all the denominations in most parts of the urbanised Western world, the guiding of God the Holy Spirit as he teaches 'the company of those who believe' to express what it means to be 'of one heart and soul' (*Acts* 4:32).

But the life of a Christian group is not always smooth and supportive. Things can go wrong—as in the life of any of its members. What are we here for? Which way should we go? Why are we so divided among ourselves? What is God saying to us? Who is to take the lead? What is our relationship with our families, our congregation, our work?

At such times, the group—and especially the group leader(s)—needs a friend beside them. Such a friend can help the group to seek its purpose in the Lord's will, listen to his voice (especially through the scriptures), learn to discern what is happening among its members, and minister in the name of Jesus Christ to his church and to his world.

In this situation, the only true Friend is the Spirit himself. The Paraclete, the Comforter, the Advocate—the New Testament titles for the Third Person of the Holy Trinity demonstrate the stand-by relationship he has with us. And usually he expresses this by anointing others as his agents, in what they are in Christ, in what they say—and in what they write.

Jean Grigor's book is one such agent. In its warm and resourceful pages, the author has brought together the teaching of the Gospel with the insights of group behaviour and downright common sense to assist us as we come together to grow to love the Lord and one another.

Many groups will find real wisdom in these pages, not only when they experience difficulties, but at any point of their life together. I strongly commend it—not just as an invaluable and readable book in itself, but because I believe it will assist the Church through its groups to demonstrate that love by which others will know whose disciples we are.

John Gunstone

Part I
INTRODUCTION

The last time he was with his special small group of friends, Jesus said to them

I give you a new commandment:
love one another; as I have loved you, so you are to
love one another. If there is this love among you,
then all will know that you are my disciples.
(*John* 13:34,35.)

ABOUT 2,000 YEARS AGO, CHRISTIAN GROUPS WERE TOLD

'Speak the truth in love'
Eph. 4:15

'We are bound to love one another'
I John 4:11

'Love must be genuine and show itself in action'
I John 3:18

'There is nothing love cannot face'
I Cor. 13:7

'We love because he loved us first'
I John 4:19

'Keep your love for one another at full strength because love cancels innumerable sins'
I Pet. 4:8

'Live in love as Christ loved you'
Eph. 5:1

'Never cease to love your fellow Christians'
Hebrews 13:1

'You should try your hardest to supplement . . . brotherly kindness with love'
2 Pet. 1:5-7

'Let all you do be done in love'
I Cor. 16:14

Have you ever belonged to a group of people who were trying to love one another?

TO THE CONGREGATION OF GOD'S PEOPLE AT CORINTH...

... when there is jealousy among you and you quarrel with one another, doesn't this prove that you are men of this world, living by this world's standards? ...

... no one should be looking out for his own interests, but for the interests of others ...

... I am told that when you meet as a congregation you fall into sharply divided groups ...

... Love is never boastful, nor conceited, nor rude; never selfish, not quick to take offence.
Love keeps no score of wrongs;
does not gloat over other men's sins, but delights in the truth ...

PAUL

(Quotes are from *I Corinthians* 3:3; 10:24; 11:18; 13:5,6)

Sometimes we look back to the times of the early church with the feeling that being part of the faith-family then must have been a perfect experience of belonging—of loving and of being loved. We contrast the struggles in our own lives to relate lovingly and to go on relating lovingly in small groups, and we wonder what is wrong.

It can be a shock to discover that Paul had to write to the church at Corinth because the Christians in that city were in a hopeless mess with their relationships! We tend to think that the glorious chapter on love (*I Corinthians* 13) was written to inspire future generations with a poetic description of what was being lived out by the Christians there. Actually reading Paul's letter, becoming aware of the fighting, the jealousies, the selfishness, the immorality, the vengefulness, the destructive anger, the power struggles of that Christian community, can give real hope for the church nowadays. If the apostle could write in that situation that the one thing that mattered in the church was love, and that love could transform that church if they were prepared to strive for it, then the very same could hold good for today.

Why did Jesus *command* his followers to love one another? He could have said, 'I would like you to love each other', or 'You'll discover that life will be fuller for you if you love others.'

We come into relationship with him and with the rest of the Christian community through faith. Faith is not necessarily costly and demanding although it can be. It is the next step, putting faith into action within the tension of the God-neighbour-self triangle, that

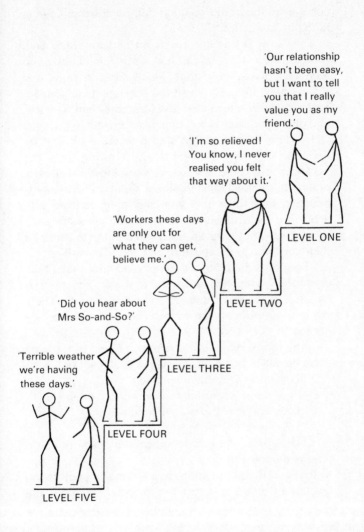

costs everything and goes on and on costing. Love is faith put into action.

The New Testament insists on personal faith and, traditionally, much stress had been laid upon good works following from that. Many congregations and many, many good Christian folk have genuine concern and compassion for those less fortunate than they are, and give time, energy and money to prove it.

It is the next step that seems to scare us. The bit about loving one another. Not just giving love, but getting some back. Not just recognising the needs of others, but actually telling others about our own needs and allowing them to try to put their concern into action for us. It involves giving up our self-sufficiency and taking off our masks. It is even offering to some for their acceptance or rejection the parts of ourselves that we find it so difficult to accept. We know that Christ died for us just as we are, and that we are accepted by him just as we are. Do we know that his love can help the man or woman next to us to accept us just as we are too?

In his book *Why am I afraid to tell you who I am?* John Powell indicated five levels of conversation:

Level five: Cliché conversation
Level four: Reporting the facts about others
Level three: My ideas and judgments
Level two: My feelings
Level one: Peak communication (absolute openness and honesty)

In our church meetings we normally operate on levels five to three. Level two greatly influences the way we report facts, the judgments we pass and the

I may have faith strong enough to move mountains, but if I have not love, I am nothing.

(*I Corinthians* 13:2)

My brothers, what use is it for a man to say he has faith when he does nothing to show it? Can that faith save him? Suppose a brother or a sister is in rags with not enough food for the day, and one of you says, "Good luck to you, keep yourselves warm and have plenty to eat", but does nothing to supply their bodily needs, what is the good of that? So with faith; if it does not lead to action, it is in itself a lifeless thing.

(*James* 2: 14-17, *NEB*)

You should try your hardest to supplement your faith with virtue, virtue with knowledge, knowledge with self-control, self-control with fortitude, fortitude with piety, piety with brotherly kindness, and brotherly kindness with love.

(*2 Peter* 1: 5-7)

ideas we hold and communicate, but we rarely share feelings openly and consciously. We find this embarrassing. It makes us vulnerable.

Small groups of people who are trying to love one another need to be able to share at the feeling level and to work towards moments when they experience peak communication. Only in this context can a person's ideas and judgments come to be accepted as part of the living, growing person that he is. If feelings are disregarded and if there is no attempt at openness there can be conflict with and rejection of a person because his ideas differ from the rest of the group.

The person who is each one of us is so much more than his opinions, his ideas, the way his personality comes across to us; further, he is so much more than his feelings.[1]

Something from the totality of what you are will call forth a unique response from the potential in the totality of what I am; and if we two are not alone, but part of a group in which each individual is recognised as having limitless possibilities for loving, then some day we might be known together as those who are disciples of Jesus.

*   *   *

1. In this book I often use the words 'he', 'his', 'him', 'himself' when it would be more correct but also more cumbersome to write 'he/she', 'his/hers', 'himself/herself'. In no way do I want to imply that caring groups contain men only!

This book seeks to fill a gap in curriculum material presently available in this country for groups who want to learn to love one another. The gap is in the field of relationship building and deepening.

As a group develops its own lifestyle there may be many meetings where there will be no set programme but simply an opportunity to share with each other the areas in their lives where they feel the need for the group's support.

The exercises which are given are designed to explore and deepen caring relationships. They are chosen so that an average group can handle them without further outside help. They are not intended to be taken in sequence, one after the other, but rather to supplement and to stimulate the on-going life of a caring group as and when they are appropriate.

Hopefully, various members of such a group would feel able to undertake in turn the preparation necessary for the group to participate in any particular exercise chosen.

Nobody is an expert in loving relationships! Together we can experience love, and we can struggle to become more loving. A caring group is a good place for growing into being the Body of Christ, so that his love might then be put into action in all the varied relationships of everyday living.

*　　　*　　　*

Part II
WHAT HAPPENS
IN A SMALL
GROUP?

SMALL GROUPS IN THE CHURCH

Everybody knows what it's like to belong to a small group. You may never have been to a caring group or a Bible Study group, or even a small committee meeting, but you will almost certainly have been part of a family, and have had experience of being with a group of friends having fun or talking together.

Being part of a group is an experience common to nearly everyone. Most people don't like being alone too much. People need people.

Perhaps the most important small group ever as far as Christians are concerned was the group of twelve men Jesus gathered round him for the time of his ministry. In *Mark* 3:14 we are told that Jesus wanted that group for two reasons: in order that he could have them as companions, and in order that they could learn to go out to preach and heal. Towards the end of his earthly ministry Jesus still needed the presence of those friends to support him in his agony in the garden of Gethsemane. Presumably, if the twelve were such a support to Jesus, they were also a support for each other and in fact continued to be so after Jesus' death and resurrection.

It was within this group setting, as they travelled with Jesus, saw him at work, asked him what they wanted to know, reported back on their experiences in mission, quarrelled amongst themselves, failed in some of their attempts at healing, misunderstood Jesus' priorities when the mothers brought their children to him, huddled together in terror after his crucifixion, ate with him after the resurrection, that they grew together in love and learned to be his disciples. It was a close group, but not an exclusive one. Sometimes womenfolk travelled with them. At one time there were seventy sent out on a mission, two by two. Sometimes those who were healed followed the group. On one occasion five thousand men plus women and children gathered round, and on another there were four thousand.

If Jesus himself chose to have frail human beings around him for support and companionship, how much more should Christians today be aware of their needs in this way! Often 'strong' Christians (and clergy are amongst these) run great risks in ministering alone to needy individuals, and develop a series of dependent relationships which become a great burden to them and prove unhealthy for those they try to help. The risk can be greatly lessened when an individual is welcomed into a small caring group, especially if that group has been learning to care for all its members.

A group is a highly powerful system for influencing the lives of those who belong to it, and through them, for reaching the lives of others.

Congregations who can have several caring groups scattered strategically throughout their parish can have an extremely effective set-up for pastoral care both for church members and, through them, for those who live around the neighborhood. Christians who live geographically near one another can have each other's love and concern at the level of practical, everday living, and neighbours will see that Christianity affects relationships and can be including in the caring should they wish or need it.

It is helpful to know a little about what happens when groups operate if you are a member of a group.[1]

In the Church, small groups of people have been coming together for nearly two thousand years, and they would appear to have done so without such theoretical expertise. This, however, is not the case! In fact, the New Testament is full of helpful advice and dire warnings in the field of human relationships.

This is written to help ordinary people harness the forces that come into play when a group meets, so that they can steer the group towards a good experience where the members grow together in love.

1. There is now a huge body of literature on 'group dynamics'—far too much for the average person who feels in need of the kind of support a group can give.

AS A GROUP IS LAUNCHED, CONSIDER THESE QUESTIONS

Why should this group come into being? The person or persons who call the group into being will have explained to those invited their purpose in forming a group, but the first meeting should include a time when all those present are invited to share their expectations of the group, and together come to some agreed statement of purpose. It is difficult at this stage to be very specific unless those invited have had some previous group experience and know precisely what they want, but if nothing about the purpose of the group is discussed, differing expectations will lead to confusion and disappointment as the group's life develops.

A group that is not meeting the needs of its members will have no good reason for staying together. Each member who plans to join should consider whether or not the stated aims of the group are such as warrant his commitment to them in the midst of all the other demands on his time.

Almost certainly, as a result of the experience of being together for a while, people will come to be able to formulate much more clearly what they want and need, so it is wise to organise for some kind of evaluation of what has gone on, together with some agreed plans for the future after the group has settled down a bit.

At the end of this book there are helps with evaluation in a group. You will be able to decide the most appropriate time to use a particular style of evaluation. (See pp. 205ff.)

What will be the nature of our commitment to each other? Any group which forms in order to enable folk better to love one another needs some kind of contract of commitment. Some married couples admit to there having been times when they would have split up rather than pay the cost of working at loving each other, if they had not been bound by the marriage vows. Because they were committed to each other they worked through the difficult times and arrived at far deeper loving and understanding than ever they had before. Group life can be just like that. Think through the following matters together:

a) how often will the group meet, and for how long each time?

b) where will it meet and why?

c) when will other commitments take precedence over group attendance?

d) will the membership of the group be closed, or will there be times when others will be welcomed at the group's meeting?

e) if this group is one of several in a congregation how will it relate to the other groups?

f) how long should the life of this group be?

There is a general tendency to start an organisation on the assumption that it will go on and on, sometimes long past the time when enthusiasm has become duty. In today's highly pressurised and mobile society it is reckoned by some that if a group is meeting once a week the members should covenant to be together for no more than nine months at a stretch, and to review the situation after that period.

*   *   *

POWER IS AT WORK IN A GROUP

> For where two or three have met together in my
> name, I am there among them.
>
> *Matthew* 18:20

> In union with him you too are being built together
> with all the others into a house where God lives
> through his spirit.
>
> *Ephesians* 2:22

There is the presence and power of the Spirit of God at work for Christians in a group. Anything that can happen in the life of an individual Christian open to the Holy Spirit can also happen to a whole group who are being built together. Remember that the fruits of the Spirit are 'love, joy, peace, patience, kindness, goodness, fidelity, gentleness and self-control.' Most of these 'fruits' make sense within relationships, not in isolation from others. Non-Christian groups also feel that there are forces in their midst when they come together, more powerful than the sum of the influence of their individual personalities. That is why the theory of what goes on in groups is termed 'group dynamics'.

The gifts of the Spirit should also be in evidence in a Christian group.

> In each of us the Spirit is manifested in one
> particular way, for some useful purpose. One man
> through the Spirit has the gift of wise speech, while
> another, by the power of the same Spirit, can put the
> deepest knowledge into words. Another by the same
> Spirit is granted faith; another, by the one Spirit, gifts
> of healing, and another miraculous powers; another
> has the gift of prophecy, and another the ability to
> distinguish true spirits from false; yet another has the
> gift of ecstatic utterance of different kinds, and

another the ability to interpret it. But all these gifts
are the work of one and the same Spirit, distributing
them separately to each individual at will.

I Corinthians 12: 7-11

In *I Corinthians* 14:12 Paul urges Christians to concentrate on the gifts which build up the church.

A group need not be engaged in theological discussion, prayer or Bible study as such for the Holy Spirit to be at work. When a member of a group shares a piece of good news, a current problem, a previously hidden fear, a secret dream, or anything of importance in his life, the group can experience the fruits of the Spirit and the gifts of the Spirit in response.

There is also a great deal of destructive power about in the dynamic of any small group. No matter how much we try to love others we seem to be far better at looking after ourselves. When we are challenged, we become defensive. Sharing is sometimes too risky for us, so we prefer to confront someone else to make them open up instead. We say something cruel or thoughtless, and we are not strong enough to ask for forgiveness in front of all the others. Someone else is getting a lot of the group's attention and jealousy creeps in. An argument erupts when we least expect it, and we feel we daren't lose face by acknowledging that the other person might be saying something worthwhile.

Transactional Analysis (TA) suggests that we can understand puzzling behaviour in people when we consider that within each person lives the little child he or she once was. That child was probably looked after by loving and well-meaning parents, but inevitably there would arise situations when even the most secure child could not cope. The little one did not have the experience of life to know how to react constructively to a situation where he was scared or confused, so the behaviour he produced did not deal with the problem of his fear or confusion, but rather made it worse. Because there was no satisfactory resolution of the problem the first time it occurred, the inappropriate behaviour was reproduced time and time again, like an old tape-recording, whenever the child pressed the panic button.

To test out this theory, think of two people in a typical group which has set out to be a caring group, to listen closely to what every group member says, whose behaviour is not always appropriate for the way the group normally operates:

Imagine a man in this group who persists in voicing his opinions without any apparent concern for the opinions or feelings of the others present. Probably you will notice that his voice tone changes when he acts like this, and it sounds either aggressive or pleading. The next time this happens in a group when you are there, use your imagination, and visualise him at three years of age. See him as a little boy who badly needs to have attention paid to him. See him trying in vain to share something of importance with his father who, tired and busy, has come home and retreated behind a newspaper. If you can do this, then respond to that three year old part of him who badly needs to be heard, understood, and appreciated. If he begins to get his needs met he might be able to stop pressing his panic button in your group.

Now imagine a woman who sits quietly and attentively, but says little or nothing although she is obviously following what is said by others and being with them in spirit. In your mind's eye, whisk her away and see in her place a four-year old being 'seen, but not heard', perhaps even being laughed at when her family had visitors for saying something the grown-ups thought odd, but which was never explained to her. That little girl inside the grown woman needs the encouragement of knowing that her ideas are just as acceptable as the next person's, and that in a group where everyone shares, her contribution will be missed. But she probably has years of believing in the keeping-quiet pattern of behaviour to overcome. Time and again she will have sat and thought something like 'It's just as well I didn't say such and such, because nobody else mentioned it.' If only she had, the conversation might have been enriched by a fresh and stimulating idea! But her childhood belief about herself did not dare allow that thought to pass through its system.

The power of the frightened child inside each group member is one to be reckoned with. It tends to be highly manipulative, and to reproduce in fellow group members the feelings and reactions of the parents of that child so long ago, whether these be feelings of irritation, sympathy, over-protectiveness, boredom, fear, or whatever.

But the power of the frightened child is not greater than the power of love available to the group through the Holy Spirit.

We must not be conceited, challenging one another to rivalry, jealous of one another. If a man should do something wrong, my brothers, on a sudden impulse, you who are endowed with the Spirit must set him right again, very gently. Look to yourself, each one of you: you may be tempted too. Help one another to carry these heavy loads, and in this way you will fulfil the law of Christ.

Galatians 6:1,2

Be forbearing with one another, and forgiving, where any of you has cause for complaint: you must forgive as the Lord forgave you. To crown all, there must be love, to bind all together and complete the whole. Let Christ's peace be arbiter in your hearts: to this peace you were called as members of a single body.

Colossians 3:13-15

If you become angry, do not let your anger lead you into sin; and do not stay angry all day.

Ephesians 4:26

If you go on fighting one another, tooth and nail, all you can expect is mutual destruction.

Galatians 5:15

SOME VERY PRACTICAL DETAILS

Where should the group meet? The atmosphere of a home is normally much more conducive to sharing, caring and the building of relationships than is the average room on church premises. These days, when the cost of living is spiralling and church buildings are becoming so expensive to heat and maintain, it makes a lot of sense for the church to go back into the homes of its members, except for times when larger groups of people will be coming together than an average living room can easily accommodate.

There are good reasons for sharing amongst all the group members the experience of being hosts to the group in their own homes. One's home is often an extension or expression of one's personality and beliefs, and so this is one way of getting to know the other members better.

As the various group members arrive at the door of the host home, the neighbours will notice that something is going on, and this may be one way to witness to them that faith includes relationships. It might even arouse an interest in them to be included in the invitation next time round. Opening one's home to a group means putting some energy into belonging, which sometimes results in a deeper commitment to the group than before. So do not hesitate to ask new members if the group can meet in their homes some evening.

In an average group, however, there will be people for whom having the group in their homes might be an embarrassment or an inconvenience. If only one member of a family belongs to the group and there is only one public room in the family home, then it might be an unloving gesture towards the rest of the family for the group to be invited to come in and take over the available space.

Similarly, if there is illness in the home, or an elderly relative who wishes to go to bed early and not to be disturbed, that group should care enough not to wish to be invited there.

Some young couples, on the other hand, would more than welcome having the group in their homes for more than their fair share of the time, because either they would require to find baby-sitters, or only one could attend the group each night.

Sometimes an elderly person does not like to go out of a winter's evening, but would love to have the group come to him. Obviously, as the group grows to know each other, settlement of these matters becomes easier.

Who should come? When you are choosing to make up groups, whether separately, or as a network, remember to include those who may be unable to attend church because of some circumstance or handicap.

Deaf persons, because their handicap is not visible, are often overlooked and misunderstood. Church worship is often difficult for them to follow. But a small group can quickly adapt, if it will, to speaking in a way in which they can follow and fully participate. With such encouragement it is possible for a deaf person to stop feeling as if he or she is a nuisance. It does require the co-operation of the deaf person to say so when hearing is limited, as well as the love of a group to remember which ways of speaking are helpful to the person concerned.

Many people have physical or emotional handicaps which make getting to church or participating as others do (sitting, standing, kneeling) painful, awkward or embarrassing, but in a small group these needs can be explained, understood and accepted.

People need people to maintain emotional health. Hopefully, any Christian group will include some people who for one reason or another have to live alone and others who, like single parents or those looking after elderly or sick relatives, receive very little appreciation from other adults in their everyday environment.

There are some people who just do not like being in a small group, apart from social occasions, and there are also some who cannot enjoy that involvement either. It is working against the spirit of love to persuade people to attend against their will, no matter how much someone else feels the group might do them good'.

Be comfortable. Modern homes are not built for large groups on the whole. Do not have more people in your group than can be seated comfortably in the room you have. Many younger people enjoy sitting on the floor, so cushions can be a good alternative to having enough seats for everyone. It is best when every person can see every other person in the group from where he or she is seated, otherwise the conversation will lose some of its personal quality.

Do make sure there is enough fresh air circulating in

the room, or people will be leaving the group with stuffy headaches. Remember when you are setting the thermostat, that several bodies in a room together raise the temperature considerably in quite a short space of time!

A matter of time. It is good to have set times for starting and finishing group sessions. If some members are on shift-work, or parents have to rush home to relieve baby-sitters, meetings that continue beyond the agreed times can stop people coming back. They can feel 'out of things' if the group normally goes on after they leave. It's not so much a matter of 'Isn't it great! Our discussion last night went on till after midnight!' but rather of loving concern and respect for those who have other commitments to honour.

What shall we eat? There is no need at all to have anything to eat or drink at a small group meeting. Some groups decide that even the time the host spends out of the group boiling a kettle is time when at least one valuable member is missing what is going on in the group.

Many groups, however, do make time, once the main sharing of the group is past, for an informal chat over a cup of tea and a biscuit. Often in Scotland the hostess will bring in a plateful of pancakes or scones she has baked to provide a cosy, family feeling in contrast to the 'church-meeting-feeling' engendered by plain biscuits. Common sense will suggest that large spreads of goodies are quite inappropriate for supper at a group meeting. Inevitably, some competition will creep in and a family might feel it has to provide at least as many platefuls as the last family, if not one extra. This is certainly out of step with witness to a simpler lifestyle and good stewardship.

Then celebrate! By all means, have celebrations. Make occasions when the group will have a party, and then let everyone who is able to do so share in providing the good things to eat and drink. Let the feast be enjoyed, and have fun with it.

In summer, have a group picnic or, if you have a network of groups in your parish, have a big picnic for all house-group members and their families.

If you want the people in the various house groups to get to know each other's families, then book the church hall and have Sunday lunch together. Heat up a big pot of soup and ask everyone to bring sandwiches to share. Organise one or two games to help people meet each other and infuse some fun and energy into the gathering.

Spread the news. If it is time to tell others in the congregation about what it means to the house group members that they have the regular support and joy of belonging to a network of caring groups, then ask the minister and the lay people who lead the congregation if you can do something one Sunday morning to spread the good news.

Use the time of the normal service to share some personal experiences of help and insight in the groups. Invite the congregation afterwards (as personally as possible) to a shared 'soup and sandwich' or 'bread and cheese' lunch. For the meal, divide those who come into small groups, each with at least a couple of house group 'regulars' for direction. After the meal, arrange to give each of the groups a good sharing experience, using something suggested in this book (see pp. 69ff), or one of your own ideas, and finish with some form of worship in which everyone can participate; it need not be lengthy. People will then have had some introduction to what happens in a house group, and may be encouraged to join.

A GROUP IS BORN

At the beginning of a group's life together, there is normally a cosy, secure, 'womb period' when all the members feel happy with each other and good about belonging to this group—it's almost a feeling of euphoria. But this stage will pass, and with its passing the group will enter into the struggle to be born: to become, not just a collection of individuals who are becoming known to each other, but a unique, never-to-be-repeated organism with its own distinctive personality.

WHAT LIES BEHIND GROUP STRUGGLES?

Especially in the first few weeks of any new group's life, there are three major questions that concern each individual in it. Generally, these are felt rather than consciously thought out.

First of all there is the big question of whether or not I really belong to this group. Am I an 'insider' as far as this group is concerned, or would my presence not be vitally missed?

Then there is the question of the 'pecking order' of this particular group and where I come in it. How much weight will anything I say carry with the total group? Will I be listened to? Will I be able to influence the others in this group if I feel strongly about anything, or will my wishes be overlooked?

Lastly, but most vital of all, there is the question, 'Does this group love and value me as a person?' Will my needs to give and receive love be met in this group? Will they care if I am hurt? Will I get enough positive reinforcement from this group to enhance my functioning outside the group and to give me strength to work through the relationships inside the group if there is any conflict or disillusionment?

For these aspects psychologists use the words 'inclusion', 'control' and 'affection' and say that we need all three in any group we belong to. One of the tasks laid upon any group working on loving relationships is to be aware of those factors.

> You must look to each other's interest and not merely to your own.
>
> *Philippians* 2:4

> We ought to see how each of us may best arouse others to love and active goodness, not staying away from our meetings, but rather encouraging one another.
>
> *Hebrews* 10:24,25

It can be a shared responsibility amongst the group to ensure that each person is included (unless he chooses not to be on any particular occasion) in all sharing, decision-making, even in general discussion. It's the task of each member of the group to learn to listen to each other person. It would be unrealistic to assume that because members are Christians we feel an equal spontaneous friendship towards each member of the group; but it is asked of us that we take the trouble to try to love, respect and forgive every other member—which probably includes willingness to change oneself just as much as wishing the other was different!

HOW MIGHT SOME STRUGGLES SURFACE IN A GROUP?

The ways for the struggles to surface are so numerous that it would not be possible to list them. Lots of little things can happen which might seem of no great importance but, when added up, mean that people are feeling uneasy.

By taking flight. A phenomenon which occurs just when a group seems to be on the edge of something with emotional overtones is that, without warning, the group will take off in a totally irrelevant direction, just as if it were flying away from the harsh reality of working through relationships.

Or perhaps someone will seem to take up more than his fair share of the group's time, in a way which appears attention-seeking to the others. Some of the group's initial eagerness to listen to each other drops; a few people lean back on their chairs, one steals a furtive glance at his watch . . . and the group splinters for a while.

Many folk, because of cosy childhood memories, enjoy being led in a group by a strong motherly or fatherly personality, and would quite comfortably sit back and become dependent. In this situation, however, none of the children looks after the parent figure; it can be a mutually unhealthy relationship for a group of adults. This is one reason why it is often a good thing for the minister of a church *not* to be a house group leader, as he or she is often expected to be Big Parent in that role.

By fighting. Small power cliques of two or three can start to gang together for support against the others, or against a dominant leadership figure. If the designated leader does not happen to be the person the group looks to for emotional leadership then at some point the group may split because of divided loyalties.

Just because group members growing emotionally close begin to feel like a family for each other, family struggles left over from childhood sometimes come into play. They can be difficult to diagnose because in today's highly mobile society folk tend to have moved from the district where they were well known as part of their families. A person will feel an immediate rapport with another person whose appearance or personality somehow reminds her, not always consciously, of a well-loved relative or friend. The opposite is certainly true. Instant dislikes are taken, and feelings of 'I could never trust a person like him' come with no logical reason for either such fear or rejection. An innocent victim can have loaded on to her the bad feelings left over from a relationship that was not properly under-stood—even a relationship made in fantasy with a storybook or television character.

Sometimes one strong individual will clash with another equally strong personality and the clash from their differing opinions can be very unpleasant for those members of the group who have painful childhood memories of parents fighting and of their own powerlessness to reconcile them.

A man who felt he had to compete with an older brother in childhood might become involved in a struggle for leadership with a man older than himself. A woman who had been the eldest child in a large family and who was given early responsibility for the younger siblings might unconsciously try to mother the younger people in the group who might in turn view her as interfering, and not allowing them to be themselves.

By adopting roles. Individuals will often adopt roles, and insist on playing them far beyond the point when others tire of their way of operating. For instance, someone can take on himself to be the group's 'joker', and be this quite acceptably for a while until the humour is seen to be a mask, or is deemed inappropriate.

There is almost always in a group some person who seems to have no opinions of his own, but is always expressing agreement with other members—a 'yes-man' role. There are many other such roles, and you will be able to spot which are being adopted in your group.

In his book *Games People Play*, Eric Berne, the originator of Transactional Analysis, wrote of three common roles people adopt with each other as they interact: Victim, Persecutor and Rescuer.

In any group there is likely to be a person who seems to enjoy being often in the Victim role, by his words and actions seeking to be put-down by the other group members. If so, there will always be a Rescuer who rushes to comfort the Victim and to offer advice even when it is clearly not asked for. And to complete the triangle they will require a Persecutor; one who will give the put-downs by sarcasm, one-up-manship or just by constant interruption. In fact, each person can play any of these roles at times of insecurity. There are reasons why people prefer one role to another, and why Victims attract either Rescuers or Persecutors. It can take a long time for a group to build up sufficient trust among its members for some to begin to relate without masks and form straight relationships.

A leader aware of such factors in a group can direct the group's attention to what is going on and ask all the members to take responsibility for changing what is happening. It is easy for people in a small group to avoid truly meeting each other; it is difficult, but so worthwhile, to go into the struggle and grow together.

People have no need to engage in psychological games if they feel valued in a group. Our loving of each other is not likely to be perfect, but if it is genuine, it begins to deal with fear.

GAMES PLAYED BY GROUPS

Eric Berne called these games 'Psychological Games' because he realised that people were often quite unaware that they were manipulating others by the way they were interacting with them. They were operating partly at the psychological level.

The only reason people have for playing psychological games is that they are feeling insecure and want to keep their distance from those threatening to them.

Since many of you who read this book will be familiar with Bible stories I will illustrate these games in progress in the scriptures in personal and group relationships:

One common game is 'Mine is Better than Yours.' *Genesis* 37 tells the story of Joseph, the spoiled and favourite son of his elderly father. At the age of seventeen he was hated by his ten older brothers, and not without cause. He began to have dreams in which he placed himself above not only his brothers, but even his parents. Another person might have kept quiet about this, but not so Joseph. His game nearly cost him his life!

It may not be nearly so dramatic when played in a small group today, but have you heard some people, before they settle down and begin to feel valued in a group, play the version which goes something like this: 'Of course, when we lived in . . .' or just 'In our last church we always . . .'?

It doesn't make for good relationships as the people in the here-and-now church or town squirm uncomfortably till someone comes rushing in with a tactful 'rescue act'. Remember that the need for such a game comes from the feeling of not belonging in the one who begins it. It can be stopped, not by pointing out that the person is playing games with the group, but by valuing him more. Perhaps that means finding out more from him about what happened at Inveruppitty and suggesting that the former inhabitant might like to show the group how it can happen here too.

Think of Martha in the short story told about her hospitality to Jesus in her home in Bethany in *Luke* 10: 38-42. Martha was a 'Now I've Got You!' player when she felt tired. The message her guest, Jesus, was proclaiming all over the country, and perhaps the very subject he was discussing with her sister Mary, was that God cares, and he had come to show that caring. Martha was slaving away in her kitchen making the best meal she could because she cared about Jesus, and what was happening? She was being ignored completely. She listened to all the warm and loving sounds of the conversation between her sister and Jesus until she reached boiling point, and then she rushed in with a remark which ought to have cut Jesus to the quick. She didn't say 'I'm tired and cross, and feeling overworked and under-appreciated.' Instead she said, 'Do you not *care* that my sister has left me to do all the work by myself?'

Martha was in the role of Persecutor, and Jesus could have played the Victim, been over-apologetic, while Mary rushed to the rescue and told Martha how wonderful it was to have a sister like her . . . But he didn't. He stopped her game by appreciating both her feelings and Mary's actions, and by not accepting the blame when blame was not appropriate.

As people come to know each other better, this knowledge can sometimes be misused by trying to hurt by prodding at another's weak spots. Other gospel stories show how the Pharisees tried time and again to play 'Now I've Got You' with Jesus, but he was a master at stopping such games. It is not a loving action to let a person victimise you, nor fair to yourself to allow another to rescue you. It can be a painful process in a group to sit back and let Victims find out for themselves that they are quite capable of looking after themselves if others corner them or put them down. People are not fragile.

Another common game is 'Yes, But . . .'. You may well have in your group kindly folk who love to give others advice from their own experience. If this is what the person who receives the advice wants, then it is felt to be good and supportive, but sometimes what a person is saying when asking for advice is, 'I'm not feeling very good about myself at the moment, and I'm not going to let you try to make me feel any happier'.

In this frame of mind the person concerned will present a minor problem like, 'I just can't do a thing about my neighbour's dog . . .' A well-meaning friend will follow up her tale of woe with,

'But why don't you keep your gate closed?'

'Oh' she will reply, 'but the milk boy couldn't get through it in the morning with his arms full of bottles if I did.'

'Well, have you thought of telling your neighbour

38

that you don't like his dog chewing your roses and asking him to keep him under control?'

'But the neighbour on the other side shouted at the dog the other day so he must know by this time that . . .'

The end of that game is that the other group members begin to feel angry and helpless, and eventually someone will be rude to the person who began it all. With that she can feel quite justified in carrying on with her unhappy feelings about herself, having collected even more evidence that 'nobody has any time for me these days'.

Moses tried that game with God, and the writer of *Exodus* took one and a half chapters to record what went on between them during it. It is told in chapters 3 and 4. It draws to a close with the telling phrase, 'At this, the Lord became angry with Moses . . .' One of the Bible studies in this book is based on that story. (See p. 123.)

If you have any group members who are keen church workers you can be almost certain that amongst them will be 'Harried' players. This is another of the games Moses played.

To be good at playing 'Harried' all you need to do is too much! Each person has his or her own limit of energy. One person can be doing the same amount of work as his neighbour, but one can be playing 'Harried' while the other is working competently and enjoying it. A 'Harried' player is one who takes on so much that he or she has not the time and energy to discharge all the commitments well and happily. Towards others such players usually adopt 'Rescuer' roles, but end up in the

Victim position, with stomach ulcers, nervous breakdowns, heart attacks, divorce—or perhaps by resigning from everything at once and feeling a complete and utter failure. Perhaps the worst times for those who stand by and watch are the in-between times when such folk are driving themselves on and on and doing everything badly, seemingly unable to stop and decide on priorities.

Moses was fortunate—he had a wise father-in-law. In *Exodus* 18 there is written the story of Jethro's visit to him, when he saw him wearing himself out, imagining that he was indispensable. As always in this game, Moses was over-estimating his own strength and under-estimating the abilities of others.

A caring group can help a 'Harried' player learn to say 'No' and to establish some priorities in his work-pattern and keep to them.

Turn to *I Kings* 18, 19 for some of the most dramatic story-telling of the Old Testament. The crunch had come in the conflict between the prophets of the Lord and those of Baal. Fire was sent from heaven, and the Lord's prophet, Elijah, was vindicated in the sight of the heathen. A tremendous victory had been won. But the very next day, there was Elijah fleeing for his very life, scared to death, because the queen had threatened him.

Into the wilderness he ran, and prayed to God to die. He did his level best to play 'Poor Me' with the Lord, but with beautiful patience the Lord's angel looked after him, resting and feeding him for forty days.

Anyone who has gone through the kind of public exposure and threat to life as Elijah did then might well be in a state of nervous exhaustion. It is understandable that some depression might come over him, but after forty days of recuperation and peace Elijah was still feeling very sorry for himself. Finally the Lord told him quite firmly that it was time to go back again to work; that his assessment of the situation (made through his scare and exhaustion) just was not true. He was not alone: seven thousand of the Lord's people were there to support him.

Sometimes a sympathetic group is just what a 'Poor Me' player is looking for! There she can sound off about never having had a chance in life, and about her unfriendly neighbourhood, and about applying for a job that was given to someone else with fewer qualifications, and about . . . and about . . . Eventually someone in the group has to have enough loving concern to do some gentle confrontation, help her face reality, and accept responsibility, while giving her the support of the Lord's people.

When a person plays psychological games in a group, he or she is usually unaware of the fact. To others, the repetitive pattern of behaviour can be very obvious. Games begin in childhood, and people are so expert at playing their favourite ones that by the time they are grown up they are second nature to them. Since games damage relationships, a group which can help love its members out of the need for playing them will do something very positive, both for relationships inside the group and beyond it.

41

FEELINGS INFLUENCE A GROUP

Human beings have feelings. A little child feels, and instantly expresses whatever feelings he has. We are left in no doubt as to whether a toddler is angry, happy, hurt, bewildered, amazed, curious or scared. Very soon, a growing child senses that it is not always in his best interests to be so open in a world where more powerful people can take advantage of his weaker moments, and so he learns to feel one way inside, and act in another way.

Our British culture has demanded that display of strong emotions be kept under control in public. There can be acute embarrassment if a man is seen to weep in front of others, or even if someone shouts and dances for joy (except as a reaction to sport!). Within our Christian culture there is a very strong disapproval of a person showing any form of negative feeling towards another person.

Amongst the most powerful forces at work in a group are the feelings that the members are experiencing inside themselves. It is entirely normal to have feelings—both positive and negative, loving and very unloving. And whether or not those feelings are expressed openly, they influence what is going on amongst the group members.

What do people do with feelings? First, they feel them! After that, they can choose what they do with them. They can express them there and then, verbally or non-verbally, and then respond to the reactions they bring from other people. If they choose not to express the feelings right away, they can let them simmer away, die down, bubble up again, cool off, and so on, until one day, perhaps weeks after the feelings first began, they say to themselves, 'That's the last straw!' and the pot boils over and someone gets hurt. Finally, they can deal with feelings by thinking about what has caused them and what is the appropriate way of dealing with them to further relationships, and then act on their thinking and feeling.

Unfortunately, because so many Christians think it is not loving to express or share negative feelings, they choose the second way, which is in fact one of the surest ways to damage relationships. Many people in groups, when their pot boils over, resign, walk out, talk behind people's backs, carry grudges against people they could have been really close to. They are defending themselves at the expense of the Christian fellowship.

A caring group can be a safe context in which to express feelings and learn more about them. One of the marks of a group that is really working on loving one another, is that it is able to express both positive and negative feelings and to work through conflicts to deeper understanding and sharing than ever before.

In the New Testament we are not instructed *not* to be angry: we are advised not to save up angry feelings, but to deal with them on the day we feel them.

A group which appears to have no negative feelings amongst its members is almost certainly being influenced by the negative feelings which are not being expressed openly.

If the group is to grow in loving, people need to be enabled to share their negative feelings, to take them

43

seriously, and have the group do something about them.

The alternative to that is that the group exists rather than lives. Its members might still feel they benefit from attending it, but it probably won't have a very great impact on their lives as Christian people trying to live the Gospel today.

HIDDEN AGENDAS

In any friendship between two people there come times when the relationship loses some of its initial excitement and goes stale. Sometimes there may be hurtful differences of opinion which make the friends want to argue and fight or to withdraw and pretend these differences don't exist. If this happens with two personalities it happens even more so in a group of eight or ten. In a group of eight, there are seven potential personality clashes for each individual, so altogether seven times seven for the total group! Each time one member is absent from a meeting of the group there is a different balance of personalities, and therefore an essentially different group meets.

All group members bring to each meeting their expectations about what they want from the group on that occasion. Although, again, this may not be a conscious decision at all. One woman may have had a very trying time with her young children and all she wants is understanding and support. A man may have been feeling he was getting nowhere with his work because of a boss and so he decides, quite unconsciously, that tonight at the group he's going to use the power he has to get some decisions made about what work the group could take on together. A teenager might have had an argument with his schoolmates about the existence of God and he can hardly wait to get to the group to pick their brains in order to knock his pals for six the next day with all the 'right answers'! Someone else may have been feeling in a bad mood, and in her mind as she comes to the group is that person who always interrupts others; if he does it again, she'll be in no mood to take it, so the scene is set for a show-down.

The expectations and motivations behind what takes place in any group are frequently called 'hidden agendas'. A good group leader should be aware of this very powerful factor in group dynamics. If he thinks a hidden agenda is influencing negatively a particular meeting he should ask the group to help find out what is going wrong. If it is acknowledged, it can be worked through.

Basically, this calls for an ability to help group members get in touch with their feelings and bring them into the open so they can be faced. If the feelings are destructive, get the group to go behind the feelings to the reasons for them, so that there can come a degree of mutual understanding and acceptance.

Another tool necessary for a group leader is the ability to spot the good and constructive happenings, and to point them out to the group. Groups consist of people, and people grow and develop healthily with encouragement and praise where it is due. The group can thus develop a pattern of building itself up in love.

OPENNESS AND CONFIDENTIALITY

It is possible to appear to be open and sharing in a group and yet to be unconsciously demanding certain conditional responses from the others that are far removed from trusting them.

If you choose freely to give away a secret you have kept to yourself, you can no longer expect to control what happens to your secret.

If you give away a secret openly then you are saying to each person who hears it, 'This is precious to me. My giving it to you means that I trust you, and will respect *whatever* you choose to do with it.'

Many groups have had a pact that its members should not 'tell another person's story' outside the group. This means that a group member is free to tell an outsider the story of what happened to herself or himself in the group, but that telling what happened to some other person is reckoned to be gossip, and thus breaks the rules of the group.

Yet with the best will in the world, if a secret is told, it may be remembered months or years later, even after that group has been dissolved. If so, a person who has remembered what was told may well forget it was shared in confidence long ago, and may pass it on.

Some people even choose to manipulate a group, perhaps unconsciously, by telling information in a way that almost dares others to pass it on. Usually this person has a past history of 'proving' that people can't be trusted. If your intuition tells you that something like that is going on, whether or not you are leading the group at the time, ask for a discussion around the area of trust so that feelings can be expressed and group decisions made around this issue.

TEARS

Once a group is operating at the feeling level, there is the possibility of someone shedding tears at the group meeting. For some people, even some leaders, this event is intensely embarrassing and so is dreaded.

Embarrassment can lead to responses like, 'There, there, don't cry', or even an awkward silence with group members attempting to avoid looking at the person who is in tears.

Often adults in our culture link tears with weakness, and will do all they can to prevent themselves and others crying—almost as if tears were a sign that the one who sheds them has failed, or is about to go to pieces!

Tears are a normal expression of sadness. If a person gets in touch with sadness in a group context, it is entirely appropriate to shed tears. It is recorded in the gospels that Jesus wept, both at the tomb of his friend Lazarus, and on the occasion when he was so moved to see Jerusalem, knowing that its inhabitants were about to reject the Messiah God had sent to them. Both of these were public occasions.

Most adults have experience of comforting a sad child. When an adult cries, the child within is sad, and needs comfort. The tears are a sign that this is so. Except with people for whom touch is frightening, an arm around the shoulder or a hand held in the midst of the tears, with no attempt to stop the flow until it stops naturally, is often the best way to help a person who cries in a group. If someone wants to say something to the person in tears he should use encouraging, understanding words which will help the tears to flow, not words to stop them.

People who have been a lot with young children know how well a child can use tears to manipulate grown-ups and even older children. Sometimes in a group, there will be a person who will still have this pattern of behaviour, although it will come over usually in a more sophisticated way. This can be far more tricky to handle than tears caused by genuine sadness.

Sometimes it is quite obvious to everyone in the group that tears are being used manipulatively, but at other times the only indication is that people begin to feel uneasy with what is going on. Good indications that tears are manipulative are that the crying goes on longer than one would expect, is done more often than is usual or in some other way demonstrates that the reaction does not seem to fit the situation.

Tears always are shed to say something. They can say 'I am very sad' and, for instance, a bereaved person who can cry in a group, might shed tears of sadness on several occasions just because of the relief of being with warm, supportive people. With someone in this situation it might be good to ask how he or she would like the group to react when the tears come. After the first or second time the person might by far prefer it if the person next to him or her gently placed a hand on their hand and the group went on with whatever was happening, giving the person the chance to feel supported but not to feel the need to stop the action in the group for any more attention. Be sure to check it out so that everyone understands what is wanted.

But tears might say something like 'Please pity me',

or 'I'm not getting my own way', or 'Nobody understands how awful it is to be me', or 'I'm helpless. Someone will have to take care of me'. All of which, with others besides, are tears of manipulation. If it seems that something like this is going on, the most helpful thing to do is to ask the person in tears what he or she is saying by crying. Let them find the words behind the tears. Sometimes people surprise and shock themselves out of such behaviour just by being gently confronted in this way. If necessary, the group can then help the person to ask for what is needed in a straight way instead of using tears to manipulate others.

A GROUP DEVELOPS ITS OWN DISTINCTIVE PERSONALITY

Everyone knows what it is like to get together with a group of friends and remember experiences shared in the past. Special words that had significance for the group are used again. These words would mean little to those who had not shared that experience.

Any group that stays together for a while builds up its own culture, and a language that has peculiar significance for its members alone is part of that. Language is an essential part of communication within a group, and if a group can build up a language around shared experience this can contribute towards warmth, understanding one another and openness.

Part of the culture of any group is the rules which evolve from its life together. These rules are not necessarily voiced, but they come to be understood by everyone in the group. For instance, a group can allow its members to gossip about others not in its membership, or there can be the unspoken rule that such behaviour is inappropriate. A group can be one where members can be trusted absolutely not to talk outside the group about what is shared within the group in confidence, or it can be a group where someone would have to be quite desperate in order to trust the others with a personal problem. A group can be a group which speaks the truth in love to each other, or it can be the kind of group which allows a member to become a scapegoat for the sins of the others, usually with one

52

person being the centre of a brutally honest attack with no love in evidence at all.

These rules are not usually decided upon by discussion, they evolve in a group, and each individual member is aware of them and operates according to his understanding of them even although he has never sat down to work them out for himself.

A healthy and loving group makes time on its agenda every so often to bring to the surface, discuss, and if necessary, change the rules which are operating within it.

DIALOGUE WITH THE GROUP

As Jesus began his ministry he began also to gather around him a group. As part of the training of his twelve disciples, he sent them out on mission—but not alone! After his death, they continued to meet together. Why was there this emphasis on support and togetherness?

Inside any individual there runs continuous dialogue. When a person is physically alone he is not psychologically alone. With him are all his images of the persons significant to him.

Perhaps this is most obvious when he leaves a friend and walks off down the street. Almost automatically his mind goes over some of the things said in the conversation. He savours again the good things to extract more positive reinforcement for himself, and he frets over whatever passed between them that was puzzling or unacceptable. And so it is as if his friend is still with him in dialogue until something else claims his attention.

Very early on in life a person is trained to engage in dialogue with her parents in their physical absence. A toddler carries around in her head a recording of her mother's voice saying 'Don't touch!', 'Say thank you', 'Be a good girl', 'I love you'. When she is left with a neighbour while mother goes to the dentist, she knows how she ought to behave.

Later still is developed the ability to dialogue with characters read about in books, or personalities seen on the screen.

And so, when a person feels he really belongs to a

group, that person can be in dialogue with the group any time he wishes.

Belonging to a group where she is loved and valued for herself can make a tremendous difference to a person's thoughts, feelings, self-esteem, and subsequent behaviour. It is no wonder that so many church people report a much increased ability to speak and act lovingly once they have begun to belong to a caring group. Even when they are physically alone, the group's love and belief in them is available to them psychologically.

Of course, we who are Christians believe this very thing about Jesus—that his Spirit is always with us, but for so many people having his Spirit embodied in a group is so much easier to understand, and so much more immediate.

A loving group can be a way in which we relate to Jesus because it is part of his Body—a part we can touch and laugh with, listen to, and love.

A group is a powerful tool for influencing values, beliefs, and actions just because of this. We carry it around with us as a living yardstick, available should we wish to use it.

THE USE OF TIME

In her book on Transactional Analysis in the church, *Born to Love*, Muriel James points out that the New Testament has two words for our word 'time'. *Chronos* is the Greek word meaning time measured by the clock in minutes and hours, or by the calendar in months and years. *Kairos* is the word used when it is the significance of the hours spent that is being discussed. One woman might say 'In 1973 . . .' whereas her friend, talking about the same year, might refer to it as 'the year I married John . . .': for one, the reference is to *chronos*; for the other, the year had a special meaning and was *kairos* time.

I have heard people say of a particular group meeting, 'That was a waste of time tonight,' and of another meeting of the same group, 'Wasn't that wonderful? Tonight I felt really close to the rest of you.'

An average group will meet for no longer than two or two and a half hours at a time, and perhaps not even as long as that. It is important to learn to use the time spent together as meaningfully as possible.

The theory of Transactional Analysis can again be of help here. It outlines several ways people structure time to get what they need from life. It gives names to these ways so it is easier to think purposefully around this subject using these categories. In any group meeting all six can be observed and experienced:

Withdrawal. A remark made by one person can set another off on her own train of thought and for a while, although she is sitting with the others, she can be far away in spirit. In fact, it is quite hard to be in a group for two hours and not to withdraw, at least for a moment or two, in this way. Sometimes the withdrawal is through boredom, but not always. It is good, even in the middle of a group meeting, for a person to follow through on her own thoughts if need be, especially if it leads to her sharing some fresh understanding with the rest.

Ritual. A ritual is a sequence of events known and familiar to those who take part in it. It is not necessarily 'religious'. Ritual can have the effect of separating a group into being isolated individuals again, not in relationship for its duration. At other times it can give a feeling of togetherness and of deep sharing.

A group will develop its own ritual whether or not this is done consciously. The way the meeting begins and ends is often ritualised. The most useful ritual is the one a group has worked on together and agreed upon.

Group leaders are sometimes at a loss to know how to stop the initial chit-chat as members gather. One group I belonged to worked out the very simple ritual for a member, chosen that evening, to open by saying 'Let's start the meeting by five minutes of silence together.' Each man or woman in that group was a busy person at home or work, and that time of quiet together was one of the most refreshing occasions in our week. After the silence, the leader for the evening would say a verse of scripture or a short one-sentence prayer, pause for a second or two, then the rest of the business would begin. That particular group normally ended by standing in a circle holding hands and repeating the benediction together before parting.

Pastimes. The name describes itself. Pastimes are what happens when people want to pass time. The chatter about the cost of living, the latest scores and Mrs McSporran's canary is usually pastiming. It's fine when a group is gathering, but is usually experienced as a waste of time if it occurs in the middle of their time together.

This is one of the times when, if the people involved have discussed some of the theories in this book or in others like it, there will have evolved a common language to deal quickly with what is happening, and without offence. If it happens when the group could be functioning at a much more meaningful level, one person could suggest, 'Are we pastiming again?' or, at the start of the meeting, the leader could say, 'Pastiming over!' and the group will quickly be available to share at another level.

Activities. These are quite intentional; they are things done in a group for a particular purpose. Under this heading will come discussion, sharing experiences, praying, reading, creating, and so on.

Games. The fifth way of structuring time in relationships is by playing 'psychological' games. These are described elsewhere in this book. (See pp. 36-41.) Since these are ways of hurting folk and putting them down they are destructive of relationships, and a sad misuse of time.

Intimacy. The TA definition of intimacy is of something that occurs rarely. It is a peak experience when people are being completely open, trusting and accepting of each other. As this is not common between two people relating to each other, it is even more unusual for a whole group to experience it together; but it can happen. It's something to work and pray for, but it cannot be organised. When it happens, it is beautiful. It is what we were made for! *Kairos* is truly experienced in such moments. It is what the Bible calls fellowship.

OUR NEED FOR RECOGNITION

Basic to any understanding of people is the knowledge that human beings need individual recognition and attention.

In one of Tom Wilson's humorous cartoons, Ziggy is sitting rather pathetically in a corner. Above him is the caption

> You don't have to be alone to be lonely . . .
> . . . but that's when you feel it the most!

The gospels are full of incidents where Jesus gave personal, individual attention and recognition to those who seemed to be without it: the woman at the well of Samaria, blind Bartimaeus, Zacchaeus, the woman taken in the act of adultery, the widow of Nain whose only son had died, the man among the tombs at Gerasa, to name a few.

'We love because God first loved us,' John wrote in his epistle (*I John* 4:19, *Good News Bible*). Unless a person has experienced love, loving others is very difficult, and loving oneself impossible.

In a well-filled church on a Sunday morning, the worshippers cannot feel that the minister is giving them individual attention every week, although it is quite possible for each person to receive something very personal from some part of the service. But in a small group it is possible to have just that, both from the leaders and from the other members.

In this book the suggestions for studies, meditations, group exercises and prayer are all designed quite specifically so that everybody will be able to participate, unless he or she wishes not to. This is because I believe that each person has a valuable contribution to make from experience, and because I know what a difference it makes to people when they are valued and given the recognition they need.

REALISE YOUR ASSETS

Part of what your particular group will do will come from outside your group. You will get various ideas from books like this one as to what you can do together. Sometimes you will respond to needs outside your group. A great many factors from outside can influence how your group will function.

One very important factor not to be overlooked is the wealth of special talent, training, circumstances, and personality characteristics that are combined in the members of your group. These, as much as anything else, should help determine what your group decides to do and be.

Let me give some examples from groups I have belonged to, or heard about:

One group member had a talent for painting, but also believed that inside most other human beings there lies undiscovered ability in this line. She offered to guide the group in a painting session one evening, and brought along prepared hardboard, some oil paints and various painting utensils. Great fun was had, and some people were encouraged to go further. Some found they could actually express their thoughts and ideas through painting at a level they couldn't manage in words.

A certain group member was an avid reader. In the group she often referred to interesting things she had read. One evening she brought along a couple of books about a subject that had been interesting the group and gave short reviews on them; the books were then lent out to those who wanted to read them.

Another person had a lot of time on his hands. He had been forced to retire early because of ill-health and often could not go far outside his own home unless someone escorted him. He therefore promised to remember in prayer daily the needs of the other members of the group expressed at the weekly meetings.

Yet another loved to take coloured slides. One evening he showed some beautiful transparencies of the countryside, with some close-ups of spiders' webs, flowers, ferns and seashells. After that he led the group in reading *Genesis* 1, with everyone joining in the repeating chorus 'And God saw that it was good.'

One member had a flair for organising. She took it upon herself to draw up rotas of those homes in which the group should meet, and when, and whose turn it would be to lead various parts of the group's activities.

It is quite exciting to discover unusual talents or experiences in your particular group and to see how they can be woven into its life.

It is even more exciting when members begin to discover their ability to do things they never dreamed they would do, because their fellow group members believe in them. Good groups generally have blossoming members!

Be flexible. If your group stays together for any length of time, then you can expect that various group members will be involved in family events like births, deaths, illnesses, mental or emotional upsets, anniversaries, major decision-making, problems of bringing up children, and those associated with elderly relatives, and so on.

Some of these are known in advance, but many will come upon people quite unprepared for them. The most natural thing if a person belongs to a group which is meaningful for him or her, is to share something of the experience—the joy or the pain or the worry—with the other group members.

No matter what has been prepared in advance for any group meeting, something of concern to one of the members of the group should be dealt with first.

No two groups can ever be identical, just because the personalities that make up the group are all different and the experiences these people pass through during the group's life are special to them, and no others have exactly the same experiences. Make the most of it.

WHO SHOULD LEAD?

If the group is one whose aim is to love one another (with all that that entails) then the essential qualities for the leadership of such a group are the honest desire to love others and the need to be loved by others.

The ability to be open, and to model the kind of behaviour and attitudes hoped for from the rest of the group is essential.

Leaders who try to be dictators work against the life of such a group, because they do not bring out the potential for loving which lies in each member. They manipulate rather than enable others.

Some groups will be led by officially designated leaders. In other groups leadership will be shared amongst the membership. Again, this is something for the whole group to work out.

Whether or not leaders are 'officially' chosen, the task of leading the group will not always rest with these designated leaders. At different times in a group's life different styles of leadership arise and are helpful.

Sometimes the group has a task to accomplish, and if one of the group has a clear insight into the steps to be taken to do this then, hopefully, this member will perform in a leadership capacity at that time. Sometimes there are several options open for a group, and at times like those a member who can collate them for the rest of the group and help the group decide on priorities is helpful. Sometimes what is needed in a group is the ability to tune in to what a distressed member is really saying, and at such times someone who can gently model the necessary encouraging concern in empathetic questions or an arm around a shoulder, should take the lead. Every possible gift of the Spirit in a group expressed by any member at the right time, can lead the group in a love-fulfilling way.

If your group has a designated leader, please remember that he or she is also a needy member of your group. Do not allow your leader to use that role to avoid relationships. Some people accept leadership to cover up their fear of being vulnerable. In a leadership role it is sometimes easy not really to belong to the group. But, whether or not this is the case, remember to love your leader as yourself too.

TRAINING

Many denominations now employ staff to give training to people involved in small groups much more personally than can be accomplished through reading a book.

Training can also be gained from secular agencies that give much helpful new insight for Christian people who will train along with others and work at adapting what they learn for use in the church.

Any courses in group dynamics, transactional analysis, self-awareness, bioenergetics, gestalt, or other such that help people listen, observe, relate sympathetically and constructively with others are worth attending under secular auspices.

Courses run by various agencies with particular pastoral concerns, such as Marriage Guidance, Cruse, Samaritans, Age Concern and so on can be of immense value to those who want to be more loving.

There are, of course, some things which can only be learned in the Christian community, like prayer and Christian meditation, the study and use of the Bible, the sharing of the sacraments, worshipping through music. And if the people of God are to discover new ways of being his church today, there is great benefit in knowing well how this has been expressed in the past.

This book is written to help train those who cannot attend such courses; to be a resource book and a reminder for those who have; to give stimulation both for those who lead groups and those who want to belong to groups effectively; and to bring some hope to those who are despairingly struggling through the un-love of so much of the church's life today.

THE THISNESS OF A PERSON

Who is the person sitting next to you? . . .

The person nearest you is a unique world of experience. Within him is constantly going on a world premiere of experiences that no person has ever had, or ever will have. He is a unique cluster of memories of the past and expectations of the future. He has some things he can do well. There are some things he can do better than anybody else in the whole world. He is the only person in the whole world in direct touch with how he feels, sees, experiences.

He is really a whole colony of persons, of inner inhabitants, of people met all during a life. Something of these people has entered into this person forever, so that the person sitting next to you is really a community . . . All the live things of this world that came and interacted with this person are still deep within.

> *Each person is this world of experiences. And when a person drops out of a group, or out of the great experiment of man, there is lost a whole universe in which many people have been gathered . . .*

He can never be fully understood. He is more than any description or explanation—or your perception of him. He can never be fully controlled—nor should be. You cannot violate him with impunity. He is one of the great mysteries you will meet in your life.

(From *Inscape,* p 37, by Ross Snyder, Abingdon Press, 1968.)

Part III
GETTING TO
KNOW YOU
SESSIONS

You cannot really love someone you don't know well, and getting to know others in a group can take a long time unless this is specifically planned.

When you ask people to share with others, choose a subject they are familiar with. The best subject for this is personal experience. Just in case you happen to touch on something a bit too personal for some people in the group, make it clear that at any time it's alright for a person to say he would rather not share.

It is important to plan for some 'Getting to know you' sessions at the beginning of a group's life, but it is also worthwhile to have similar sessions once the group is well established, because in them people suddenly see other dimensions in fellow group members that they hadn't even guessed were there!

NAME TAGS

If the members of the group do not know each other's names when they come together for the first time, suggest they each make themselves a new style of name tag. Give to everyone a large blank sheet of paper and a felt tip pen. Ask them to write:

i. In the middle of the page the name they would like people in this group to call them.

ii. In the top right hand corner their favourite meal.

iii. In the top left hand corner the place they would like to be if they were not in this room right now.

iv. In the bottom right hand corner the names of two people who have had a great influence in their lives.

v. In the bottom left hand corner what they would grab first from their home (apart from people) if their house caught fire.

vi. Then, round about their names, five words ending in '-ing' which describe their personality.

Next, you need a supply of ordinary pins so that each of the group can pin this to his front!

Now invite the group to stand up and circulate around, getting to know each other via the information on the name tags. This stage can take as long as you allow it, so it may be good to say beforehand how long you want to spend on the exercise. When they have all done this you might like to sit again and share your feelings about the exercise.

If you want to you can structure this by inviting the group to share their answers to questions like these:

i. The person I learned most about in the last few minutes was .... because ....

ii. I was very surprised to learn .... about .... because ....

iii. I have discovered something in common with .... because ....

iv. I have discovered that .... and I are very different, because ....

Note: This exercise is very easily adapted. Decide on whatever you think would be fun for your group and help them to get to know each other better and use your own ideas instead of the ones suggested here under items i-vi.

RECENT EXPERIENCES

Another 'Getting to know you' exercise is to ask everyone to share some recent experience with the group. Make it specific, for example:

a) The thing that gave me most satisfaction last week.

b) The happiest experience I had last week.

c) The best news I have had recently.

d) The most exciting thing I am looking forward to.

e) The recent news which caused me most concern.

I suggest that you do only one of these subjects on any given evening, unless you particularly want to choose, say, two contrasting ones. Again, add your own ideas to the list.

MONTAGES

This one rather makes a mess, which will have to be tidied up, but it is good to introduce another way of communicating into the group apart from spoken and written words.

Before the group arrives there should be gathered a huge pile of old magazines, newspapers, pamphlets, crayons, scissors, felt-tip pens, odds and ends, sellotape, glue and, for each person, a blank sheet of paper, as large as possible.

During the meeting, everyone is given his blank sheet and asked to make a picture of himself (not of what he looks like, but of the person he is) from the material available. People should feel free to hunt through the magazines to find words or pictures that convey something about themselves, to cut these out and stick them on to their sheet.

When the montages have been made, each person should offer his picture in turn to the group and the group convey to him what they see about him from his picture. After that he will have the chance to fill the rest in on what they did not pick up.

Note: If you would like to do this without the mess, and at a deeper level, ask the members of the group to make their montages at home and bring them to the meeting. Because they have a week to think about how to present themselves and what they want to communicate, the results are often much more complicated and therefore encourage sharing at a deeper level. On the other hand this much more sharply defines the difference between those who are good at this sort of thing and others who have felt hopeless at art since schooldays!

PERSONAL COAT-OF-ARMS

On an evening when you have plenty of time
—about fifteen minutes for each person in the group is
required—you could use this sharing exercise:

Give out blank sheets of paper and pens. Ask
everyone to draw, as large as possible, a blank heraldic
coat of arms, something like this shape:

Suggest that
they then
section it off
and number the
sections as in
this diagram. (It
would be good
if you had a
clear model to
show them
exactly what
you meant!)

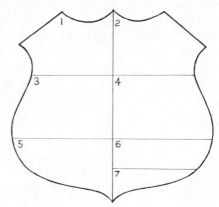

Tell them that either words or symbols are used in
heraldry to convey significant details of a person's life
or family background, and that they are to use either
words or symbols to fill in each section as you tell them
what is required. Inform the group that at the end of
this individual filling up of the coat-of-arms, they will
be asked to share the content with the group (unless
any choose to opt out of any particular section).

Give them the instructions for each section and allow them to complete it before you tell them what goes in the next one.

Put down:

– in section 1, two things you are good at.

– in section 2, your greatest achievement so far.

– in section 3, your family's greatest achievement.

– in section 4, your most significant religious experience.

– in section 5, how you would spend your last year if you were told tomorrow that you had only one year left to live.

– in section 6, two words you would not like people to use about you.

– in section 7, two words you would appreciate people using about you.

After everyone has completed his coat-of-arms, then use all the rest of the time for sharing what has been put down. It is quite good to take one section at a time and to go round the group sharing this before you go on to the next section. Alternatively, you can ask the group to choose which sections most interested them and deal with those first, and so on. Depending on the time available, the group should draw its members out a bit on what they have put down so that they come to know each other at a greater depth than a mere reporting back would allow.

WHICH IS YOU?

This next exercise is a bit of fun, but it can reveal a lot about how people feel about themselves and how they see others. It goes better if the people in the group have already had a few meetings together.

Before the group meets, prepare twelve pieces of paper or card on which are written clearly enough for everyone to read, the following (or your own selection of something similar, e.g., biblical characters).

A. Tiger, gazelle, squirrel, panda

B. Daisy, orchid, dandelion, thistle

C. Eagle, penguin, robin, seagull

(If your group is familiar with biblical characters, you could include a series like Peter, Jezebel, Ruth, Thomas.)

Round One. To do this exercise, place one series of four words on the floor in the middle of the group and say that you want everyone to choose the one that is most like him or her. When everyone has chosen, share the choices with the whole group. Then ask everyone why he chose what he did. (It would be normal to discover that two people had chosen the same animal, but for widely differing reasons.)

Round Two. Repeat the steps for round one, with another series. After everyone has shared what they have chosen, ask all the others to write down what everyone has chosen and then why they imagine that person chose that flower. You should then take one person and go round the group saying 'Why do you think John chose a daisy?', ending up with asking John why he did actually choose a daisy. (Here is where what other people think about you begins to emerge!)

Round Three. Repeat again with your final series, but this time each member of the group is asked to write down the names of each other person and opposite the one they expect them to choose from the selection. After that they choose their own. The sharing this time involves one person being selected to get feedback. If this is Mary, then the group in turn should tell Mary which label they have given her. At the end of that, Mary will say which she chose for herself. And so on round the group.

After all that your group will have enough material to keep them going for hours on the labels we give others, how we don't know what other people are thinking and feeling but we think we do, and so on.

PRESENT CONCERN

Most people who think about life as they live it have at any given time a topic that is very real to them, something to which they come back and back until they come to some kind of resolution as to what to do, or where to take their stand.

It can range from 'Should we take my father-in-law to live with us?' to 'What am I doing with my life?', from 'I'm worried by the stories my four year old is telling me as if they are real: is she deliberately lying to me?' to 'I'm so involved in church work that my teenage son never sees me: where do my loyalties lie?'

To have the chance of sharing such a worry with a group that cares is a major help to some.

This is the kind of topic a group could start on one evening and only manage to hear out two of their members because of the depth to which the exploration of the matters can reach.

The function of the group on such an occasion is quite specific—it is to help the member concerned think through the issue for themselves, and to lend support and encouragement.

Rule 1: Do not give advice on the basis of what you did years ago or what you have heard at second hand. No two situations are quite the same. Give 'advice' only if that is wanted and only then if you are an authority on the subject!

Rule 2: Listen. Try to listen not only to the words but to the feelings behind the words. Listen, too, to what the body posture of the member is saying! But *listen*; listen very carefully. This is of great importance to the person who is sharing.

Rule 3: Ask questions. Ask them to clarify the situation in your own mind if you need this. Ask the kind of questions which will indicate to the speaker that you are understanding and supporting his thinking. Ask questions to open up another relevant area of thought, but in such a way that your question can be treated like a 'red herring' if that is how it seems to the speaker. Never ask a question to trap the speaker or to prove your own point.

Rule 4: Try to get into the speaker's shoes to feel what he might feel, but remember they can never be a perfect fit!

Rule 5: Be aware of areas of strength and love in the person who is talking and give him positive feedback wherever you can. If someone is being reassured authentically about his own capacity to deal with the problems he is facing, it is a fact that he will be more capable of working them through than if he is not sure how he is coping.

Rule 6: If there is any action the group can take as a result of the thinking through of the problem, then contract to take it. This is where loving can cost!

TELEGRAMS

One very useful technique for a group which is trying to think something through succinctly is to try to put the substance of what it wants to say in the form of a fifteen-word telegram.

If the group had been in operation for some time and felt the need to review its purpose, then each group member might be asked to compose a telegram using not more than fifteen words to tell a neighbouring church, or the people of the parish, or the local newspaper, or whatever other group was pertinent to the situation, the good news about the group's life together.

When everyone has completed his individual telegram, invite each member to read his aloud. When all have been heard, the task of the group then is to write another telegram, this time a group effort, pooling the good ideas in the individual offerings!

At the end of that, when the group telegram has been composed, there remains a curiously relevant question for the group: 'Did the way in which our group operated as we composed the group telegram actually reflect the message the telegram conveys?'

Note: If the word 'love' comes into the telegram, it might be salutory to read together the relevant verses from *I Corinthians* 13!

THINGS I LOVE TO DO

Some evening when the group has arrived tired and a bit dispirited, hand out sheets of paper and pencils with the following instructions:

Draw a line down the centre of your page.

Now down the left side, spacing them out over the page, put the numbers 1-20.

Now sit comfortably and let your mind drift pleasantly to think of all the many things you really love to do—no matter how ordinary or how important.

Make a list of them all, one below the other, opposite the numbers. (It doesn't matter what order you have them in.)

When everyone has completed that, ask them to draw lines to make the right side of their sheet into eight columns.

1. At the head of the first column put the letters M/F. These stand for Mother and Father. Go down your list and imagine what your father or mother would have had on their list had they been doing this exercise. Any item that you think would have appeared, mark with their initial: M or F.
2. Head the next column with the initial of your spouse or a very close friend. Now put that initial beside any of your items which might have appeared on your spouse's list.
3. In the third column, put a £ sign. Go down the list and put that beside any item that costs money for you to enjoy doing it.

4. Head the fourth column with A/P. This stands for 'Alone' or with 'People'. Go down your list and put A, P or both beside each item.
5. The fifth column should be headed U. 'U' is for 'Unconventional'. Mark with 'U' any item you think other people would be unlikely to have as something they really enjoy doing.
6. The sixth column is labelled N5. Mark that way any item you would not have had on your list five years ago if you had written it then.
7. In the seventh column put the numbers 1-5, labelling in order of preference the five things you most enjoy on your list.
8. For the final column, write beside each of the first five favourites marked the dates on which you last did them (as accurately as you can remember).

Now have a good look at all your columns. Tot them up and see what they say about you as a person. Share as a total group what you have discovered or had reaffirmed about yourself. (I think some of the items on the list might be as well kept a secret, but it's up to you.)

20 Things I love to do	M/F	S	£	A/P	U	N5	1-5	Dates
1. Walk with a friend in the moonlight	M	S		P			3	Last summer
2.								
3.								

SPIRITUAL PILGRIMAGE

Have paper and pen ready again for this one. When people arrive give them a sheet and invite them to draw a map, a graph or a maze; some kind of pictorial or graphic representation of their spiritual pilgrimage till now.

When everyone has completed the exercise, let one member offer his, and thus 'show and tell' his story, while the rest of the group supports him and asks him relevant questions. Do this till all in the group have shared their experiences.

At the end there will be many common elements to the stories people have told and there may well be material from experience which will be relevant for discussion on the mission of the church for today, or similar themes.

LOVE IS . . .

Have you seen the Snoopy book called *Love is walking hand in hand*? If you have, and can get a copy to show your group, you would understand this exercise very quickly. There are other similar ones in the series.

The idea is that if you want to explore any one word topic at a particular meeting, you should invite all the group members to write as many definitions as possible in an allotted time, beginning with the words 'Love is . . .' if it's love you are going to discuss, or 'Christmas is . . .' if it is near the festive season, or whatever you want everyone to think about.

This exercise is best done if the group members can be funny, imaginative and serious too, and can write a variety of definitions from their own experience. These are then shared.

LONELINESS

One of the main reasons why people want to belong to a group is to counteract the loneliness which most people experience from time to time. Of course, being alone is not necessarily loneliness. When loneliness is really experienced something happens to a person's feelings of self-worth; so such experiences are not lightly shared with others. This again is only for groups where trust has been growing.

Ask the group to close their eyes and try to imagine that they are alone in the room. Then ask them to remember times when they had been, not necessarily all alone but very lonely. Ask them to recall the time when they had been most lonely of all, and leave a few minutes' silence for them to recall this experience.

Have papers and pencils ready and follow this by asking everyone to write down their definition, 'Loneliness is . . .'

After these are shared and discussed in the group, invite the group to share their loneliest experience one by one.

It's important that this is not rushed through, but that each person is really listened to, and understood. It may be that for some loneliness will not be far off in the past but still a fear or a present reality in which the group can give support.

MODELLING FEELINGS

This is also something for when the group members have built up some mutual trust, and are beginning to share more freely.

Borrow from the nursery Sunday School a large supply of plasticine and the boards the little ones use when they are modelling it. If you want to be more adventurous, get real clay instead if there is someone in the group that knows how to handle it. It will be advisable to have hand-washing facilities and even some handcream for afterwards!

Give each group member a lump of modelling material about the size of a man's fist if you have enough to go round, and a piece of hardboard or plasticine board to work on.

Ask them to get in touch with a feeling they had very strongly——if possible in the past week. When they are feeling the way they did then, ask them to work with the material in their hands to represent the feeling in some way. Reassure them that it does not require to be a work of art. The normal reaction of some will be to say they cannot do that kind of thing. My experience so far has been that even those with very little artistic talent or imagination can do something if they can recapture how they felt, so don't let them off the hook!

When all the models are complete, ask the members to offer their *objets d'art* one at a time to the group. When a model is presented the group should look at it carefully, try to pick up the feeling from it, and then say aloud the feeling they get, if any. When everyone has spoken who wants to, the modeller can then share with words what he was communicating in clay, and the group can go as deeply as time allows into the situations that caused the feelings in each individual. Make sure everyone's model is seen and talked over.

THREE WISHES

Another exercise which can be very personal because it can reveal so much about those who choose to reveal their dreams, is this one.

People are asked to imagine they have a fairy god-mother who could grant them three wishes.

- one wish for the world,
- one wish for the church,
- and one very personal wish just for yourself.

Give the group time to think and write down their wishes before any is shared, so that everyone does his own thinking and everyone has something unique to share.

Have a time of sharing with the group, allowing the group to get to know its members better at this level.

Finally, invite each person to look over his list again. Tell them that fairy godmothers have gone out of style and they have to make their own dreams come true! Ask everyone to write beside each wish any practical step, no matter how small, that they could take, either alone or with the support of this group, towards the realisation of those dreams.

FIGHTING...

In the Introduction (p. 8) John Powell's five levels of conversation were mentioned. It happens sometimes in a group that two or more people will get into a very heated argument on the level of opinions. This can result in the people concerned growing more and more determined to win the argument at no matter what cost to relationships. Near the start of their difference of opinion they cease to listen to each other. While their opponent is speaking they use this time to draw breath and think up what they will say next. Their opinions are not being hurt in this process, but their feelings are, and so are those of the rest of the group. Someone in the group needs to stop the argument by raising the conversation to the feeling level where it belongs. But how can this be done?

One of the onlookers in the group can be honest enough to state how he is feeling as the fight rages. If this is authentic, he can tell the opponents that he cares more for their relationship than for one of them to win an argument about opinions. He can ask the rest of the group how they are feeling, and if they are honest, the replies might well be along the lines, 'I'm bored'; 'I'm scared. I don't like arguments.'; 'I feel I'm wasting my time'; 'I'm confused'.

One of the best ways, not just to stop the argument, but to get to the feeling level and restore the relationship, is to get those who were arguing into a 'listening exercise'. This is an exercise which could be done with the whole group at a meeting prior to any arguments, in a setting where the group divides into pairs, and the pairs find a subject about which they differ and use this exercise to talk it out. (See next page.)

FIGHTING: LISTENING EXERCISE

Ask one of the pair to present the first part of his case on the subject under discussion. When he has presented this, his opponent is then asked to paraphrase what he has just heard him say—to put it in his own words—to make sure he has heard it correctly. If the first person agrees that he has heard correctly, then the second man may go on to present the initial argument for his opinion. Before his opponent can reply he must restate in his own words what the second man said, and get the all-clear for that before the next point is made. And so on. What normally happens is that, because they have begun to listen to each other, they have begun to understand and feel for each other too, and so gradually they know why the other person is talking as he is, and they can come to a compromise, or agree to differ and respect each other's right to hold his own opinion.

FIGHTING . . .: 'I FEEL . . .'

Another possibility if a group member intervenes to stop an argument is to invite the arguers to sit very closely, facing each other, where they can look each other in the eye as they are talking. He then will ask them to have a conversation with each other, speaking alternate sentences, with each sentence beginning 'I feel . . .'

If one of the arguers uses the word 'feel' where he should more correctly have used the word 'think', then he should be asked to start another sentence in its place. (e.g. 'I feel you don't know what you're talking about' is really 'I think . . .'. A feeling word like 'angry', 'sad', 'confused' should follow the word 'feel').

This exercise normally gets the opponents to realise what their argument was doing to each other on the relationship level, and if they are serious about loving each other, this should be enough to change the situation and help them repair the damage.

FIGHTING . . .: 'AT THIS MOMENT, I FEEL . . .'

If any member of a group begins to feel during a group meeting that things are not going helpfully for all concerned, then it would be good if he were to invite all the members of the group to write down (if that is convenient) how they are feeling at that moment. It is quite good to put down more than one feeling word because quite often there are conflicting feelings going on inside people and that is why they have kept silent, not being quite sure whether or not to intervene. After the words have been thought, and written, they can be shared in the group and the group can then decide whether to continue as they were before or use the new data as a basis for change in the programme.

Note: If people are fighting in a group it is not much help to attack them for what they are doing. They are already feeling bad and are on the defensive. This would serve only to bring in more aggression and negativity.

Part IV
USING THE BIBLE

THE PURPOSE OF THESE STUDIES

The Bible is an inexhaustible treasure house, and for centuries it has been used by folk in many enriching ways. The biblical studies in this book have been written with two main aims:

1) to deepen the fellowship of small groups by opening up new areas of sharing and caring for each other.

2) to begin to train these groups in pastoral caring, so that their loving might come from understanding hearts.

These are not Bible studies designed to help people know the Bible. If they were, that in itself would be good, but there are many such studies outlined in other books which are much more ably written than the ones I could write. (See the selected bibliography, p. 223). The studies in this book are planned to help folk *grow to love*.

HOW TO USE THESE STUDIES

Please do *not* use these studies one after another on a weekly basis. Each one is written around an area of concern in the lives of people today. Use a study because it is relevant to what is happening (or what could helpfully be happening) in the lives of the members of the group, or to those for whom they care.

Much more could be shared about each of the subjects than is provided for in this book. These studies are designed simply to open up a subject and to discover the resources in the group which are pertinent to it. If your group needs more information or guidance than the study supplies, then contact someone who can help you more with this particular subject, and arrange for some of your group to read it up at the local library and share their discoveries with the others.

CAN PEOPLE CHANGE?

▶ Read together the story written about Zacchaeus, the rich superintendent of taxes for the city of Jericho. *Luke* 19: 1-10.

This is a well-known gospel story, and if your group is a church one, most of the members will have listened to sermons preached about the little tax-collector who changed so radically in his attitude to money because he met Jesus.

▶ Have ready a large sheet of paper and a felt pen. Divide the sheet into two halves, one marked 'Before' and the other 'After'. Invite the group to write words on the sheet which describe Zacchaeus as they perceive him, before and after his encounter with Jesus.

▶ Ask people now to spend some time just thinking quietly, on this: 'Has there been any time in my life when I changed radically?' (The change does not need to have been for the better, nor does it need to be along religious or moral lines—the purpose of this question is to point to the fact that change is possible.)

▶ Take time to allow some who wish to do so to share something of how and when they changed.

How does change happen?

* Why does a person change?

* Why did he change yesterday and not two months ago?

* Why does someone decide not to change, or not to change yet?

▶ Discuss these three questions in your group for a short time.

Background Information:
Some people in the business of helping folk to change attitudes and behaviour today say there are three factors necessary for change to take place:

1) motivation—a person must want to change.

2) permission—a person must allow himself to feel 'this is right for me now'—'today I can do it'.

3) protection—change is always risky if it is radical; usually there is some fear of unknown or unexperienced behaviour or attitudes, so it is necessary to look for support or encouragement or some major benefit to accompany the change.

▶ Take a closer look at the story of Zacchaeus' change:

* What could be his motivation to change?

* Did Zacchaeus get his permission to change from Jesus' belief in him?

* How did Zacchaeus protect himself against changing his mind again the following day?

▶   Now spend a few minutes while each person in the group works alone on this question: 'Is there some behaviour or attitude I would like to begin to change in my life today?'

▶   If so, ask yourself,

*   What would be my motivation for changing?

*   What would I need to do to give myself permission to begin today?

*   What protection would I need as I take the first step?

*   *   *

In the gospel story, Zacchaeus told the group around him exactly what change he had planned in his behaviour. The caring concern of a support group for change to happen is continually being proved in groups like Alcoholics Anonymous, Weightwatchers and so on.

▶   Invite those who wish, to share with the group any decisions they have made.

▶   As people share, have some method of praying for them there and then. For instance, after a sharing there could be

a) a time of silent prayer for that person.

b) one other person could offer a short audible prayer, and the group could join in by saying 'Amen' at the end.

c) the group could be invited to gather round that member and each lay a hand on his head, back, arm, shoulder, as a symbol of 'being fellow members of the Body of Christ.' At the same time, those who wish could pray a short prayer aloud, or give a text of scripture or a word of love and encouragement to the person who has just shared.

FREE TO BEGIN AGAIN

Background Information:

The passage for Bible study this time is a letter originally written to a house-church leader of the first century.

One of the social problems of the early church was the fact of slavery. There seems to be no outcry in the New Testament against it, but it must have presented difficulties when master and slave found themselves to be brothers in Christ. In his letter to the church in Galatia, Paul had to write:

> There is no difference between . . . slaves and free
> men . . .; you are all one in union with Christ Jesus.
> *Galatians* 3: 28.

We can conclude that someone was making some difference in their status in the church, or there would have been no need to write that.

In the letter Paul wrote to Philemon (who appears to have been a house-church leader in his town), he approached very delicately the fact that Onesimus, his runaway slave, had now become a fellow Christian and that he was asking him to forgive him. Not only that, but as a mark of forgiveness, he was asking that he take him back into his household, and begin to relate to him as brother, as well as slave. It cannot have been easy.

▶ Read together the whole book of Philemon, after having read the introduction to it in the *Good News Bible*.

▶ Spend a few minutes in the group discussing what reaction Paul might have feared getting from Philemon to his request.

▶ Spend another few minutes discussing how you would have felt had you been Philemon.

▶ And then share how Onesimus, the slave turned Christian, might have felt about going back to the man from whom he had run away. (Since Paul had to write for him, he cannot have thought he could go back completely on his own merit.)

A PROBLEM FOR THE CHURCH OF TODAY

Today, the problem does not exist in this form, and it is difficult for us to imagine how it might have felt to be a slave or, indeed, to be master to a slave.

So let's translate it into something which happens today with increasing frequency.

▶ Consider this case study:

A man of 26 has gone off, leaving his wife of 25 with three young children: a daughter of three and twin sons of eighteen months. He had gone into marriage unprepared for the responsibility of rearing a young family and as the children came along, and his wife continually responded to their demands, and not to his, he had felt that all he was there for was to bring home the pay packet. He didn't want to go to bed with an exhausted wife, and be wakened in the middle of the night with babies teething. He wanted his freedom, and a good time. So he left.

After having had some of that 'good time' he wanted, he came in contact with a prison chaplain, and through him, became a Christian. During his absence, his wife had found some support in joining a local house-church group. It happened that the prison chaplain knew the minister of that church, and wrote to him on the man's behalf to see what could be done about a reconciliation.

The minister went to visit the young wife and together they decided to share the situation with the house-group the following evening.

▶ Imagine that you are that house group. Share and discuss:

*   What variety of feelings might the young wife be having about the situation?

*   What feelings might the husband be having?

*   There has been no direct approach by the husband, since the request came via the prison chaplain and the minister of your church. What can your group do in this situation

  – for the wife?
  – for the husband?
  – for their reconciliation?
  – for their future together as a couple and as parents?

*   Has this case study said anything to the group about any real situation with which you may be familiar?

OLD AGE

Background Information:

Certainly in the Western world people are living longer now than they did previously, which means that an increasing percentage of the total population is over retiral age. It is good that some have so many happy years with comparatively good health after retiral, but for others prolonged existence is something to be dreaded.

When Jesus was only eight days old, Mary and Joseph took him, as the custom was, to the temple in Jerusalem to present him to the Lord. In the temple they met two old people—Simeon, a priest, and Anna, a prophetess.

▶ Have the group read together about Simeon and Anna in *Luke* 2: 22-38.

Share and discuss:

* What do you see in the lives of these two elderly people that you would like to have when you reach that age?

* What else do you hope to have or be as you grow old?

* What are your fears about growing older?

* What are you doing with your life now (whatever age you are) to prepare yourself for the kind of old age you hope for?

*   What provisions for the elderly are made

    a)   in your community?

    b)   by your church?

*   Are these adequate? If not, is there anything your group can do individually or as a group about this?

Note: This appears to be a very simple study, but hopefully it will open up an area which should be of increasing concern to those who care about other people.

There are many agencies particularly concerned about the needs of the elderly—for instance Age Concern in Britain. Family doctors, health visitors, social workers, and many others are concerned, but overworked, and are normally only too relieved to discover any individuals or groups who will maintain a long-term involvement with even one elderly person on a regular basis.

Even if the elderly folk you know are fortunate enough to be living with some of their family, they may appreciate greatly some interest taken in them from outside the home.

> For when I was hungry, you gave me food; when thirsty, you gave me drink; when I was a stranger you took me into your home; when naked, you clothed me; when I was ill you came to my help, when in prison, you visited me.
> . . . Anything you did for one of my brothers here, however humble, you did for me.
>
> *Matthew* 25:35,36,40, *N.E.B.*

DEPRESSION

Reading Psalms 42 and 43 together in the *Good News Bible* sounds a bit like listening to someone in Britain with 'New Town Neurosis', as it is popularly known! The psalmist is in exile: nothing is the same as it used to be.

▶ Have the group read through both psalms and make a list of all the things the psalmist is missing in his new place.

Background Information:
When major changes come about in a person's life or circumstances, there is very often an emptiness caused by the lack of attention or recognition he has grown used to, from the people around him, and from the various activities he normally engages in.

▶ Make another list together, of times in people's lives when they might feel just like the psalmist did. (Your list might include the following: bereavement, retirement, children leaving home for the first time, a woman giving up work to have her first baby, etc.)

Discuss and share:

* Have you ever felt this kind of empty depression?

* If so, what brought it on for you?

* How did you get out of it?

Like Humpty Dumpty, he couldn't put himself together again . . .
not yet, anyway . . .
and into the shattered void, crept depression.

▶ Now look again at the psalms and find the words of hope and encouragement that the psalmist had to keep repeating to himself.

* Discuss: why do you think he wrote them down three times instead of once?

It is a very common Christian experience in circumstances like these to feel that God is very far away and unavailable. Having other Christians say, 'Have more faith!' or 'Commit it all to the Lord and he will give you his peace and his joy', isn't much help—in fact, it can add feelings of inadequacy as a Christian, and guilt to the depression.

A good example of how God looked after someone with a depression like this, is found in *I Kings* 19: 1-18.

Background information:

For some time, Elijah had been the centre of a nation's attention as God's great prophet. He was surrounded both by supporters and by enemies—life was full and exciting. He won a tremendous victory over the prophets of the heathen god (called Baal, or Baalim in the plural), and as a result the heathen Queen Jezebel threatened to have him murdered.

Elijah, the great prophet of the mighty God, fled to the wilderness, lay down under a tree, and prayed to God to take his life there and then. Elijah was thoroughly depressed.

▶ Read the story, and find out how God took care of him.

Discuss and share:

* What did God take care of first? (verses 5-8)

* In his love for Elijah, God gave him

  a) something quite specific to get on and do (verses 15, 16)

  b) people to support him while he did it (verse 18)

  Look these up and comment on them.

If there is someone in your group who feels sad or depressed, or someone for whom your group is concerned in a situation where depression seems likely:

▶ Work out *with* that person (not *for* them)

  * Are you taking care of yourself right now? (good food, enough sleep—all the things which supply normal energy to the body).

  * Is there something meaningful you could get on with to help you stop living in the past and move into the present and future?

  * What support can we give you during this time? (This will be a combination of what the group can realistically offer, and what the person concerned can accept and find helpful.)

Comment:

This kind of help is not the wind, the earthquake, or the fire, but it can be the soft whisper of God's voice speaking through his Church.

110

Note: This study is not designed for people who are suffering from depression which needs specialist psychiatric or psychotherapeutic treatment.

If anyone in your group, or known to your group, is suicidal or is finding it a strain to cope with normal everyday living, please encourage him or her to visit the doctor for help.

If, however, a person is being given treatment for depression either as an outpatient, or in a psychiatric ward, there is still much the group can do in the way of support: listening to them, praying, being with the person, including them where possible in ordinary family life—just valuing them at a time when they find it difficult to value themselves.

A very helpful booklet in which a Christian writes of her experience of depression and of what supported her through it is *Depression*, a Falcon booklet, published by IVP.

The filmstrip *Herb the Husky* by the Church Pastoral Aid Society, is also a good tool to use if one of your group has had to be taken into hospital, and if you want to find out as a group how best to understand, relate to, and help your group member through this experience.

▶ It might be good to make up a list together of 'Dos' and 'Don'ts' for a guide to the group as a result of reading the booklet or sharing the sound-strip together.

If, of course, you have someone available to your group with some expert knowledge of depression to guide you, so much the better.

GUILT NEEDS FORGIVENESS

Note: Most protestant churches today have little in the way of structure for dealing with guilt apart from general prayers of confession or prayers from the pulpit phrased in a way the minister thinks might be helpful.

Feelings of guilt, whether real or imagined, can affect not only a person's spirit, but can trigger off psychosomatic illness where, at a deeper than conscious level, the guilty person punishes himself by becoming mentally or physically ill.

I believe there needs to be more provision for dealing with guilt in the church, and at least something of this can take place in small groups.

As trust builds up in the group, it may be that a member of the group will be able to share some guilt with the others and the group will be able to help him or her work out what to do to deal with the guilt in some form of reparation or reconciliation. The group will also be able to pray with the person for forgiveness and to reassure the person concerned of God's total understanding and forgiveness. This is part of what is called 'the priesthood of all believers'.

A study like the one which follows may also help.

▶ Have the group read two passages from the gospels:

1. *Luke* 5: 17-26.

Discuss and share:

*   Why do you suppose Jesus said to this paralysed man 'Your sins are forgiven', instead of 'Get up and walk'?

*   Note that this seems to have been something done by a 'caring group' of four, for a mutual friend!

2. *Luke* 7: 36-50.

Discuss and share:

*   What might have happened before this meal at Simon's house that would cause the woman to come to Jesus like this?

Background note:

Jesus said to both the paralysed man and to the woman in Simon's house, 'Your sins are forgiven', but in neither story is it recorded that they made any public confession of what these sins were. On both occasions the forgiveness was given in the presence of a group of people. On both occasions the persons concerned knew they needed forgiveness.

Because of the above information, the following method is suggested:

▶   Give out paper and pens around the group.

▶   Invite all who wish to, to write on the paper something for which they want to ask forgiveness. It can be something they have kept as a guilty secret for years. Assure everyone that no one will see what they have written.

▶ Have a fireproof bowl or tray—a baking tray would do—and place it in the centre of the group with a box of matches.

▶ Now invite each person to ceremonially burn what they have written, thus symbolically offering it to God. Do this in silence.

▶ When everyone has done this, the leader might say, 'Where two or three are gathered together in my name, there am I in the midst', and then read a verse which promises forgiveness, such as 'As far as the east is from the west, so far has he removed our transgressions from us.' (A meditation which might be useful is on pp. 184-5.)

▶ After more silence, have a time of sharing what people are thinking and feeling, having taken part in this ritual of confession and absolution. Someone may feel he or she wants to share with the group what was written on the paper, and if so, listen to it and react lovingly and acceptingly in the situation.

FORGIVE US ... AS WE HAVE FORGIVEN ...

Background Information

In the prayer Jesus taught his followers, he told them to ask for the same kind of forgiveness from our heavenly Father as we give to others. (*Matthew* 6:12) A very sobering thought!

Have you ever said of someone, 'I'll never forgive him!'?

History is littered with individuals, families, clans and nations who refused to give forgiveness to those who had wronged them, and of lives taken or ruined in consequence.

The story of the Prodigal Son (*Luke* 15) is a beautiful example of a father giving complete forgiveness to his son without even waiting for a full confession, and of the elder brother who had kept his resentment hot over the years since the younger one left.

▶ In the group, read that story again.

Share and discuss:

* Do you find it easy to forgive people who wrong you?

Background Information:

One of the most common human failings is to carry resentments from childhood into adult life. In fact, there are very few people who do not.

The little child has a very limited understanding to cope with what happens to him. It is for example, often a complete mystery to an under-five, even if it has been explained to him by adults, why his mother deserts him, leaves him with relatives or neighbours, and then returns with a baby who seems to have taken his place in her affections. He has to make some sense of it, so he blames someone—commonly the baby, and can harbour such resentment, allowing it to affect the relationship for decades. The elder brother in the parable could have been collecting resentment against him for years before the younger one took off with his share of the inheritance. The resentment against his brother had even spilled over into resentment against the father, whom he blamed for never having given him a party when it is quite obvious that he had not communicated to the father his desire to have one.

Resentment, or 'unforgiveness' in a relationship, is like wearing spectacles which distort vision. It is impossible to love one's neighbour and have some matter for which you cannot forgive him.

▶   Invite the group to think back over their individual lives, and to remember an incident from as early in their childhood as they can when something happened that made them very unhappy . . . something for which they still blame someone else for neglecting them, or misunderstanding them, or hurting them in some way. It might seem of no great importance now, but if you have remembered it until now it means that there still must be some unforgiving attitude inside you.

When you remember the incident as well as you can, think:

*   What actually happened?

*   How old would you be at the time?

*   What else was happening in your family then that might have had something to do with what happened to you?

*   How do you imagine the people in the incident felt about you?

*   How do you remember feeling about them at that time?

▶   When you have thought this through, share it, either with the whole group if it is small, or divide the group into twos or threes for the sharing.

▶   As the story is shared, and the feelings and resentments of the little child are re-experienced, the task of those others listening is to help the sharer to think through to some adult explanation of why this might have happened to a little child like that.

▶   After that has been done for everyone who wishes, issue everyone with a pen and paper.

▶   Suggest that each now writes a letter to the person they have been holding the grudge against, forgiving them, and asking their forgiveness in return.

Note: Why write a letter?

To suggest the group members do this is to invite them to actually put into words what might until then have been merely an emotional reaction without much substance. Words need more thought, and so the feeling can be made much more specific and conscious.

Some of the letters might well be sent after the group meeting as a means of reconciliation, or the contents may be voiced when the persons concerned meet face to face.

Some of the letters might be extremely difficult to formulate because they may be being written to people who are long since dead. But this can be a method of working through pent-up grief to an experience of being forgiven that is tremendously releasing. It might well mean a lot of tears in the group—forgiving and being forgiven are both emotional happenings.

▶ After this, some members of the group might wish to share something of what they have written. If so, good; if not, that should be quite acceptable.

▶ If the group members have taken part in this freely, there will probably be little time for more, but if there has been any lack of such childhood memories for some, it may be possible, if there is trust in the group, for some to share a recent situation where they have found it difficult to forgive someone, because they do not fully understand the situation. If so, sharing that in the group might mean that some of the group members might have suggestions that will help the one who shares to understand a bit more of what could have been behind the other person's actions.

► If this happens, the group should then support the person who has shared, to find some way to begin a reconciliation with the person concerned.

TRUST AND GUIDANCE

Background Information:

Trust is of the essence of the Christian faith. It is part of loving God and your neighbour. It is easy to have a theoretical discussion on trust and to sing about it in church, but this exercise is designed to help you have a first-hand experience of the extent to which you exercise trust in other people and how much you need to keep control of everything yourself.

▶ Begin the time together by asking folk to complete some sentences like

1) I trust people when . . .

2) People trust me if . . .

3) Trust involves . . .

4) For me, 'Trust in Jesus' means . . .

▶ Ask them not to share their sentences but to put them away till later.

INSTRUCTIONS FOR A TRUST WALK

▶ Invite them to get into pairs and decide who will be 'A' and 'B'. Make sure that each couple has at least one wrist-watch between them, and that it is in the possession of 'A'.

Tell them that for the next ten minutes 'A' has to guide 'B' while taking him for a walk with his eyes tightly shut. He is responsible for 'B' and so should try to give him as positive an experience as he can, with plenty of variety and excitement!

At this point it would be as well for the group to discuss whether or not they should be able to go out of the house where the group is meeting, or if there are any out-of-bounds areas (e.g. rooms where children are sleeping) or any persons who should be warned not to be alarmed to see couples leading each other around! (Most passers-by are far more amused than alarmed!) Try to get the group to agree to allow couples as much freedom as they wish to take.

Perhaps a few hints and warnings might be helpful e.g., if you are the leader and are about to guide your blind partner towards stairs, mention whether the stairs go up or down. See how many different things you can safely guide your partner to touch and explore with his eyes closed. If you are the 'blind' partner, you share with your guide the things you notice: light changes, sounds, smells.

'A' has to keep the time and at the end of ten minutes, wherever the couple happens to have reached, the roles should be switched so that 'B' becomes the guide with the watch and 'A' has as good an experience as he has given 'B'.

By the way guiding can be done with voice, or touch, and perhaps a combination of both to experience the difference. At the end of twenty minutes the couples should all have returned to the starting point, and the experience can be evaluated. Be especially mindful to share the feelings of the members both of leading and of being led.

▶ Having taken time for everyone to share what he or she wants about the trust walk experience, ask the group to read together *John* 10: 1-16.

Discuss and share:
* Does the experience you have just been through, highlight any of these words of Jesus for you? If so, which, and how?

* If you have had any experiences in the past of being led by Jesus share them with the group if you wish.

* How would you know personally when you are being led today by the voice of the good Shepherd?

* Is there any matter about which you feel you want guidance today? If so, you might like to share it with the group. You might find that some in the group will be like the voice of the Shepherd for you, or might at least widen the alternatives from which you can be guided.

* Very often sheep blindly follow the sheep in front, completely trusting to be led in the right direction. Has trust in Jesus got anything to do with trusting his other sheep as far as you are concerned?

▶ Now invite everyone to find their original definitions about trust, to change them in the light of their experience if they wish, and then to share them with the group.

FACING RESPONSIBILITY

Some of the most outstanding leaders have been people of great humility. It seems there is a difference between humility and opting out of making the contribution in society which you are equipped to do.

▶ Before you do the Bible study together, have members of the group do some thinking about themselves. Supply each with pen and paper and invite them each individually to write down the following things about themselves:

1. Make a list of the major life experiences you have been through: e.g. bereavement, illness, making and breaking relationships, motherhood, etc.

2. Put down any training you have had for specific jobs or tasks: e.g. learning to drive, Sunday school teacher training, college course, evening class, etc.

3. Make a list of things you do well or enjoy doing.

▶ After giving some time to think of each of the items on the list, but not enough time to get bogged down in great detail, suggest that each person folds his paper and puts it away to be referred to later in the discussion.

▶ Now turn to the Bible passage: *Exodus* 3 and 4: 1-17. (If you are using a modern version then it will be effective if the entire group takes on to read the narrative parts and two group members—not necessarily males—are prepared to read the parts spoken by God and Moses.)

Background information:

At this point in history, the Israelites were being kept in cruel slavery by the Egyptians. In a miraculous way, Moses had been kept alive through his infancy and, though born an Israelite, had been brought up in the Pharoah's palace, and given the training of a prince. As a young man he had tried to right the injustices he had seen round about him, but had been forced to flee for killing an Egyptian. He had then spent time in the desert raising his family and providing for them by keeping sheep. He was admirably trained for the task God had for him to do—but he had not thought of all his experience in this way. It's a fine thing to be humble, but Moses was not being humble, he was being blind to his potential to do something about the situation which had been a concern to him.

▶ Now read right through these chapters to discover how Moses reacted to God's call to him.

Note: In the notes in this book about group work theory, there is a description given of psychological games (see pp. 36-41), which are ways of relating to people when one is under threat. These are damaging to relationships and mutual respect. This story is a good example of the game, 'Yes, But' . . . If your group knows about psychological games, they might get more out of this study. If not, it will still be meaningful.

Discuss and Share:

* How often does Moses give a 'Yes, but . . .' reply to God?

* How does God feel eventually about the way Moses is treating him?

* How does this kind of interaction take place today between man and God? Can any of the group say from their personal experience?

▶ Now take out the lists you wrote at the beginning of the study.

▶ Suggest that everyone throw his list into the centre of the group and then take someone else's list from the central pool. Read it, and think—'What might be expected from a person with this background and experience?'

▶ Take time to jot down a few notes of your thoughts on the back of the sheet you have taken.

▶ Now place the sheets back in the centre again, and let each person find his own and read what is now written on the back.

▶ If anybody wants to clarify anything he does not understand, invite him to ask the person who made notes on his list to talk with him in front of the group.

▶ (If the group is large, break into smaller sub-groups for this, but if not, stay in the main group.) Invite each person to share his reactions to what has been written about him.

Suggested endings:

– In silence, pray for the other person or persons who shared in the small group with you.

– Ask whether anyone in the group would like to be prayed for specially because of any challenge he or she might have encountered in the study.

– Have a time of silence in which people are invited to think of just one subject around which they often play 'Yes, but' with God. Each should then be invited to contract with the group to stop doing that from now on. The contract should include what he will do instead of playing 'Yes, but'.

THE USE OF POSSESSIONS

Note: The New Testament has a lot to say about this subject. Much of the teaching of Jesus, both in parables and in straight talking is about attitudes to possessions. Stories about the rich young ruler and Zacchaeus and the widow who put two of the smallest possible coins into the temple collection, are all on the same theme.

In the west today we are used to living with far more than we need. Television newsreels showing refugees from floods in India, for example, carrying all their worldly goods with them, are meaningless to us because we have no experience to use to allow us to feel along with them.

Is it possible to be a Christian and to have what we have? Many are now convinced of the necessity of having a simpler lifestyle, and are witnessing through it.

Somehow 'money' or 'possessions' are highly emotive subjects—people react with strong feelings when these subjects are discussed. Perhaps it is because deep down we link either our worth as persons or our chances of survival with how much we own?

I suggest that by attempting to deal with this subject at an academic discussion level, unexamined feelings will be exerting a strong influence on the apparently emotionless statements people will make. Try to tackle it first, therefore, at the feeling level, and then it will be possible to arrive at more honest objective decisions.

▶ Read together the story as John tells it in *John* 12:
   1-8.

Bible background: Similar incidents are recorded in
Matthew 26: 6-13 and *Mark* 14: 3-9. There are one or
two differences in detail, so I have chosen to use
John's version because he mentions Martha, Mary,
Lazarus and Judas who are all characters familiar
because they appear in other gospel stories. It is easier
then, for dramatisation, to get into a character if you
know something about that character beforehand.

   The one thing John does not have, which both
Matthew and Mark do, is to record immediately after
this story the decision of Judas to betray Jesus, and
the fact that he was to be paid for doing so. (*Matthew*
26: 14, 15; *Mark* 14: 10,11.)

▶ Suggest that the group dramatises the story and
   allocate parts. Each person who does not have a
   named part can be either one of the other disciples
   or another guest at dinner.

▶ *Discuss some practical details* For instance, is it
   possible to have the guests reclining on the floor in
   the room where your group is meeting? If so, it
   will be easier for Mary to reach Jesus's feet. If they
   are under the table as they would be in our culture,
   her action will be unseen, and very difficult to
   carry out! If possible, give Mary something like
   scented handcream or body lotion, so that the
   scent, as it did then, can actually fill the room.
   Check out with the person who will take the part

of Jesus that it is alright for him to remove his shoes for the dramatisation!

▶ Give the group a few minutes to think themselves into the parts they will act. Suggest that they use their own words as the action takes place, but that when it comes to the place where the words used are recorded in the gospel, that they should relate closely to the original but sound as natural as possible.

When the acting finishes, have a moment or two of silence to let its impact sink in.

Then ask each named character: 'How did you feel in the role of X?' and 'Did anything come home to you in a new way?'

After that, ask those who took un-named parts if they have anything to add from their experience of taking part.

De-role people, by saying that they can now come out of their parts and assume their normal identities. (If this is not done, it is possible to have the odd situation continuing throughout the session when people will still feel as if they are the characters they acted in the dramatisation!)

Share and discuss: (if it hasn't already been covered adequately)

* How did you feel when Mary poured the expensive ointment over the feet of Jesus?

* How did you feel when Judas objected to the action and said that the ointment should have been sold and the money given to the poor?

129

Note: These two questions are deliberately phrased 'How did you *feel* . . .' and not 'What did you *think* . . .' Make sure *feelings*, not opinions, are shared at this point.

To ponder as individuals:

* When did you last give lavishly out of sheer love and gratitude as Mary did?

* Mary may have done this on impulse, but she may also have planned it, as it was done in her home to a guest at a meal which, clearly, was planned and prepared.

Is there a gift you have been meaning to give, but have never got round to it? If so, make up your mind what you are going to do and plan when you will do it. If you need more prompting, share your idea with someone else in the group and have them ask you at the following meeting if you have done what you planned.

* Have you been saying recently about somebody's way of spending money, 'What a waste'? If so, examine your motives. Have you some vested interest in the matter, or are you being completely objective?

▶ Share your thoughts with the group if you feel they are worthwhile.

*   How were you personally taught to regard money and possessions?

- Can you remember what your father and mother said to you when you were small about these subjects?

- Did you have any specific experiences, either good or bad, that changed your attitudes?

- Do you have any method or rules you follow in giving away money or possessions to others today?

▶   Share whatever of the above you feel is worthwhile telling the group.

▶   Spend a few minutes in silence, and then share your thoughts if you wish on:

*   Is there any decision I wish to make about money or possessions as a result of this group session?

GRIEVING

Obviously, these studies will be extremely emotional for some, if not all, in the group. Why then, should they be attempted?

Grief is an experience people cannot avoid. Those who study human feelings and behaviour say that many physical and psychological illnesses are the result of people not working through the normal pattern of grieving. It is absolutely 'normal' to experience all the emotions highlighted in these studies and more besides. If folk do not know this they can feel very ashamed, for instance at being angry with God, or might bottle up their guilt feelings and thereby punish themselves for something entirely understandable—but which they think no one else has ever felt before.

The range of feelings we go through is not for those who have died, but for ourselves who have to go on without our loved ones. Feelings unexpressed can grow out of all proportion. Feelings shared, accepted and understood can be worked through constructively.

Being part of a loving and supportive group has helped many people through a time of tragedy. Sometimes it is enough just to know that someone cares—that one is not alone in a big bad world. With others there comes a tremendous relief from being able to express guilt or anger and still be accepted and valued by others. Still others need to have shared with them that their fellow members have felt similar feelings without going crazy, or being ostracised by friends, or cut off from a loving heavenly Father.

In some ways these studies are designed to lead group members into situations where they are forced to make exciting discoveries about their own rich resources for caring.

There are reasons for this. First, there are no 'right answers' to questions like how a group ought to help a young mother cope with her guilt over the death of her daughter. The best solution always takes into consideration the personalities involved, and an outsider cannot know these. The other main reason why I make no attempt to supply answers is that it would not be good for a group to have a short-cut through the struggle to deal with the situation. I believe that out of the struggle to deal lovingly with the situation, wisdom and understanding and compassion are born. Easy answers are usually trite and in no way can stand alongside the pain of grief.

Miracles of new life and fresh insight can be born from the most terrible sufferings, but they are rarely handed to us on a plate. When you have dealt with your own grief, you are free to stand beside others in their grieving.

All anyone can say is that love is the one power that really can change such a situation, and love expressed and experienced will bring hope and new beginnings.

Jesus said: 'How happy are those who know what sorrow means for they will be given courage and comfort.' *Matthew* 5: 4 (J.B. Phillips' translation).

Grainger Westberg in his helpful booklet *Good Grief* says,

> Our promise is that faith plays a major role in grief of
> any kind. But not in the way some people think. They

often seem to have the idea that a person with a strong faith does not grieve. He is above this sort of thing. Moreover, these people imply that religious faith advocates stoicism. They might even quote the two words from Scripture, 'Grieve not!' They forget to quote the rest of the phrase in which these two words are found: 'Grieve not as those who have no hope.'

Note: Occasionally people do need professional psychiatric help to work through their grief. If you find that someone in your group seems to be acting irrationally or taking too long to readjust to normal living again, please encourage that person to visit the doctor.

If, for instance, you find that bereaved persons are not looking after themselves or those dependent on them, or if they seem to be out of touch with present reality, or if the guilt they are feeling is growing larger instead of easier to live with, these are signs that they need help.

It is common for a bereaved person to have poor physical health especially in the year following the death of the loved one. If even minor ailments show themselves, do encourage that person to seek medical attention. Sometimes the physical weariness that follows the strain of nursing or even being with a dying person can lower resistance both to disease and to fear of discovering similar symptoms to those surrounding the death of the loved one.

If you have a bereaved person in your group, take time to check out about general health, not in a fussy, but in a caring manner.

GRIEF AND GUILT

Note: Deep in the heart of 'folk religion' there still lies the myth that tragedy and suffering are inevitably connected with the sin of those to whom they come.

Often in connection with a death the phrase is heard, 'What did I do to deserve this?'

Because of this, many people find reasons to give themselves guilt feelings in connection with grief, and so punish themselves miserably on top of the normal suffering due to their loss, which is enough for most people.

Perhaps 'folk religion' beliefs like this linger on because it is somehow easier to believe in a judgmental, punishing God than a God of grace and forgiveness, for sinners like ourselves.

This is one area of belief where the Old Testament and Jesus differ radically.

▶ Invite the group to look at an Old Testament story, then at what Jesus said about this subject.

Read together *2 Samuel* 12: 15-23 after you have given some background information to the incident.

Background Information:

The story of David and Bathsheba is quite well known and can be read in *2 Samuel* 11. Not only did David commit adultery with Bathsheba, but he arranged for her husband to be killed in battle so that he could marry her. After the birth of their son, Nathan the prophet told David that because he had sinned, God would punish him by letting the baby die. There follows this moving story of David trying to repent sufficiently for God to change his mind and allow the baby to live.

Discuss and share:

* What are your feelings about this story?

   Now look and see what Jesus said on this subject.
▶ Invite the group to read *Luke* 13: 1-5 and *John* 9: 1, 2.

Discuss and share:

* What for you is the difference between the Old Testament and the New Testament view of the connection between fatalities and the sinfulness of those to whom they happen?

* Are there any times when you would link a person's sin and another person's death (or his own death)?

Note: In writing this study I want to make it clear that I think David did wrong both in relation to Bathsheba and her husband. In spite of his being king, he had broken God's commandments seriously. I can well believe that people in those days linked the death of the baby with David's sinfulness. One possible connection I can see between what happened and the baby's death (but this is my fantasy) is the state Bathsheba must have been in discovering she was pregnant as a result of adultery (which could have meant being stoned to death), and then hearing that her husband had been killed in battle. Since she became eventually the mother of the wise king Solomon, presumably she would be highly intelligent herself, and would be able to guess that her second husband, David, had organised the death of her first one. It is quite possible that she had little will to live during her pregnancy, and very little desire to mother the baby born in such a way. Such psychological factors could weigh against the survival of a little one in times when the infant mortality rate must have been very high.

▶ As a group, consider these short case studies:

A.   John's wife had been in a coma for a week as a result of a car accident. In spite of the doctor's advice to try to sleep, he had insisted on being with her every night since it had happened, sitting by her bedside, holding her hand. On the eighth night a good friend managed to persuade him that he would need to sleep or he would be unable to go on. Between the time of his leaving her bedside and being driven home, his wife took an unexpected turn for the worse, and died without regaining consciousness. John refused to forgive himself for not being there when she died, and in fact died himself a few months later, although he was only fifty years of age, and had been normally healthy until his wife's accident.

B.   Beth was finding a new self-respect and freedom through studying at home for an Open University degree. An essay was due and she finished it at five o'clock on the final day for posting. Although she didn't normally allow her nine year old daughter to cycle down the main street near rush hour, she gave her the essay to take to the post office there and then and hurriedly began preparing tea for her husband arriving home. Before tea was ready, a policeman had arrived at her door. Her daughter had been killed instantly just outside the post office. The mail van had reversed into her cycle without warning.

Discuss and share:
*   If Beth or John had been members of your house group, how would you have helped them with their feelings of guilt in the midst of their grief?

*   In your bereavement experiences, have you ever had feelings of guilt? If so, were you blaming yourself for something you ought to have felt guilty about, or were you blaming yourself for actions (or lack of actions) that the dead person would well have understood and forgiven?

*   If you have had such guilt feelings, how did you deal with them?

GRIEF AND ANGER

When something bad happens, it seems to be a part of human nature to look around for someone to blame. If we are hurt, we want to hurt others.

Background Information:

The first king of the combined kingdoms of Judah and Israel was Saul. David had been chosen to succeed him long before Saul was killed.

Saul's son, Jonathan, had been a very close friend of young David, but Saul had turned against David and tried to kill him.

The first chapter of the second book of Samuel tells the story of how David hears of the deaths of both Saul and Jonathan.

▶   In the group, read *2 Samuel* 1: 1-16.

Share and discuss:

*   Which emotions does David show in verses 11-12?

*   Which emotions are described in verses 14-16?

*   In the light of what the man told David in verses 6-10 was David's a 'reasonable' reaction, or one brought on by grief?

▶   Now invite the group to look at how Martha reacted initially to Jesus when she met him after her brother Lazarus had died. Read the story in *John* 11: 17-21.

* What do you imagine she was feeling then?

Share and discuss:

* If you have ever had a bereavement, have you ever felt emotions like these?

* If so, were they against the loved one who had died,

   against someone else,

   or against God?

Note: Part of grieving is the feeling of complete frustration and helplessness that death sometimes causes. You cannot will a person back to life again. Death is final and irreversible, as far as this life goes.

With feelings of frustration and helplessness, come feelings of anger and blame. It is not 'rational', but is a normal, ordinary reaction for people to experience.

C.S. Lewis, a very prominent Christian writer, wrote about his experience of grieving for his wife who died of cancer, in a short book called, *A Grief Observed*. In it he tells of times when he railed against God, calling him 'a spiteful imbecile'.

Share and discuss:

* If someone you know is grieving, and feeling extremely angry and resentful, what might you do to help?

* If any of you have had this experience, share what helped you.

GRIEF AND DESOLATION:
LIFE'S MEANING LOST

Background Information:

One of David's sons was the lad Absolom. He grew up to be a very attractive leader to many of David's subjects. Eventually he expressed his rebellion against his father by leading the country into civil war. But David loved him, and his response to the news of his death is heart-rending.

▶   Read it together in *2 Samuel* 18: 31-19: 4.

Discuss and share:

*   Have you ever felt like this in bereavement?

*   If so, how did you manage to pick up the threads of life to weave them into a meaningful pattern again?

To experience the death of one's own child is to be confronted with one's own mortality.

*   What are your fears about your own death? If you can, share those with the group.

GRIEF AND HOPE

Background Information:

When King David's infant son died, he said,

> I will someday go to where he is, but he can
> never come back to me.

(*2 Samuel* 12:23)

Belief in life after death sometimes begins to make sense to a person only after a bereavement experience. Somehow it makes sense to believe that the loved one still exists somewhere, in some form; it is unthinkable that the spirit in a person suddenly ceases to exist just because the body can no longer function.

People who have not had the experience of someone close to them dying can be highly sceptical of someone who shares experiences like the following:

'I can't explain it, but all of a sudden I knew my husband was standing behind me. Of course, I couldn't see him, but he was there. The night before I had been terribly upset in bed—it seemed so empty some-how—but that evening when he was with me, I got such a feeling of peace! I've been a lot better since then. It's as if he came to tell me he was alright, and I could begin to enjoy living again.'

or

'One day I decided I would go to Mum's grave. I hadn't been able to face doing that since her funeral. But I went, and I sat down on top of it, and I just talked to her. I cried a lot, but I felt close to her. I needed to tell her so many things . . . you see, that's been the worst bit of missing her . . . thinking, "Oh, I must remember to tell Mum that," and then realising again that I couldn't . . . that she is dead . . . That keeps happening to me still. Well, I sat there anyway, and I just told her all I wanted to tell her. Somehow I'm sure she was listening and understanding, the way she used to. I felt quite exhausted after it, but it was a big relief too.'

These women are not tampering with spiritualism —they are grieving and coming through from desolation to hope.

> Grieve not as those who have no hope.
> (*1 Thessalonians* 4:13)

▶ Share the information given in this study and the two quotes above with the group.

▶ If anyone in the group has had a similar experience he might like to share it.

▶ Read together the words of Jesus to his followers in *John* 14: 1-6.

Share and Discuss:

* What do you feel about these words of Jesus? Do they comfort you? If so, in what way?

* If a member of your group has been recently bereaved, and at a meeting said, 'I want to know where X is now, and what is happening to him', how would you respond?

* How much do you, personally, need to know about life after death, and how much do you feel you can take on trust?

143

REBUILDING LIFE AFTER LOSS

The book of Ruth is only four chapters long, and in a version like *The Good News Bible*, the story is simple, direct, and very beautiful.

Background Information:

As this story is written, the heroine is Ruth, one of the few women mentioned in Matthew's genealogy of Jesus and, surprisingly, a Gentile.

For the purposes of this study, however, the main person to understand is Naomi, Ruth's mother-in-law.

Naomi, as the story begins, has been bereaved, not only of her husband, but also of her two married sons. She has been living more than ten years in the land of Moab, to which both daughters-in-law belong. In those days, life for a woman in such a position would be even harder than it would be today, but Naomi began a series of moves to re-create a meaningful environment for herself again, and in doing so, helped her daughter-in-law Ruth, to do the same.

▶ After giving the group the background above, have the entire book of Ruth read through in the group at a sitting to get its total impact.

One effective way to do this is to choose a narrator to read the main narrative, and choose others to read the words assigned to the various characters in the story.

If you do this, you will need to cast the following:

Naomi – widowed mother-in-law to Ruth

Orpah — the widow of Naomi's first son
Ruth — the heroine of the story, and widow of Naomi's second son
People of Bethlehem — some women and some men
Boaz — a close relative of Naomi's late husband
The workers in Boaz's harvest fields
The man in charge of the workers
Another closer male relative of Naomi's late husband.

Discuss and share:
* In chapter 1: 20 and 21, Naomi explains to her old neighbours in Bethlehem something of how she feels about her bereavements. What is your personal reaction to her feeling this way?

* Many people use such feelings as an excuse for not living life fully again. What did Naomi do?

* Naomi could have been very much alone. Where did she find support and company?

* How much do you think she brought this about for herself, and how much was merely good fortune?

Background information:
In his book *Crisis Intervention: Studies in Community Care*, Dr. Ken Morrice writes: 'One basic necessity in grief-work is the recovery by the bereaved person of the emotional investment he made in the loved-one; he needs to draw this emotion back into himself, as it were, so that he may have it to reinvest later in another person or part of his life.'

* Do you think Naomi reinvested her emotions?

* If you have been through a loss experience in recent years, have you completed your grief-work by emotional reinvestment?

* If not, how can you do it?

Can the group help you in this?

Note: Although the example given in the book of Ruth is of bereavement, getting over many other forms of loss can have a similar pattern. Your group might like to discuss this concept by broadening it out to include situations like:

— loss of a job (retirement or redundancy)

— loss of an organ, a limb or a faculty or ability through illness or by operation

— loss of friends/home by moving to a new town or country

— loss of companionship through divorce, separation, children leaving home, hospitalisation, and so on.

Part V
WORSHIP IN A
SMALL GROUP

WORSHIP AS PART OF THE GROUP LIFE-STYLE

Most Christian groups will find it good to worship together as part of the group's on-going life. There are all sorts of exciting possibilities for this and scope for experimentation and variety.

It is best to have some firm decisions made on this subject early in the life of the group, but it should also be an area constantly open to spontaneity and to review.

One such decision might be that every time the group meets there will be some worship, however short. A little ritual can give form or rhythm to a regular meeting. For example, always opening with a short time of silence, or always finishing by saying together the benediction.

TRY SOMETHING DIFFERENT

In some house-groups, worship can be a mini version of a church service. If this is what is wanted by the group, then it's good to do it just like that. However, just because the numbers, and the settings and the purpose of formal church worship and a house church group are so different, worship can be different too.

It can certainly be far more personal than in a large number, and in a group where sharing is part of the culture, worship too can be a shared experience, where everyone is involved.

Because matters can be talked over in a small group and accepted or rejected, new ideas are easily assimilated. Factors like times of silence, or physical contact, or the use of writing during worship, can be experimented within an atmosphere where a member can easily say 'I'd rather not', or 'How about doing it this way for a change?'

'THE KISS OF CHRISTIAN LOVE'

Greet one another with the kiss of Christian love.

(*1 Peter* 5: 14)

What do we do in the Christian church today about this?

This seems to have been largely translated into the ritual of the minister shaking hands with the congregation as they leave the service, or into what is called 'extending the right hand of fellowship' at services where people join the membership of the church.

Some denominations now regularly include a physical expression of 'the kiss of peace' within a eucharist celebration which is exchanged even with complete strangers, but of course, with those who are brothers and sisters in Christ to each other.

In our culture touching among adults is often interpreted sexually, and is therefore taboo, except between relatives or very close friends. Some people regard physical contact with disgust, and others find it quite frightening.

Within the church, however, we belong to the family who claim God as Father. Viewed in this way, some physical expression of family affection is quite appropriate, unless it gives offence to other members of the family.

Members of house groups very often develop acceptable ways of expressing their love and concern for each other physically. As they begin to share at a deep level it becomes quite natural to give each other a warm hug or a kiss in loving greeting.

1. *Holding hands round the group.* As they pray together, holding hands around the group can become a symbol of their unity before the Father.

2. *A group hug.* A big 'group hug' can be a natural response to a member sharing something deeply with the group. It is a response that can be felt at a different level than ever reached by sophisticated words. (For a group hug, one or two people are in the very centre of the hug, while everyone else throws his arms around the persons in front—like the petals on a rosebud.)

3. *Passing the peace.* 'Passing the peace' (where one person holds his hands with palms together while the person beside him places both her hands around his clasped ones and says, 'Peace to you', and so on round the circle) can be very meaningful and supportive.

4. *Hand on shoulder.* After a session where every one has shared something of himself with the others it can be helpful to ask that each person place his right hand on the shoulder of the person sitting next to him, and in a short silence, pray for that person in particular, remembering what he has shared in that meeting.

5. *The laying on of hands.* When a group develops into a deeply caring and sharing group its members will feel free to bring to the group those areas of their lives and relationships with which they need help and support. Just being able to share, with the group really

listening, caring and trying to understand, can be of immense support. Some groups add another dimension to this: that of the laying on of hands. Recently there has been a revival of the gifts of the Spirit in many established denominations and groups, and as a result some people feel it laid upon them to enter into the healing ministry as the result of receiving the gift of healing. The reference here to the laying on of hands is not for that situation. There may be no one in the group who feels that he has received such a gift; and yet something happens when a group cares enough to express in this way its love and confidence in the love and power of the Spirit, who is the source of healing and strength.

It can be done very simply. After a person has shared that he needs wisdom, power, guidance, health, love or other help, the group can invite him to sit where the rest can gather round him easily. He should then relax, opening himself up to receive what he needs. The rest of the group should each place hands on whatever part of his body they can easily reach, especially his head, shoulders, back, arms and hands. This can be done in complete silence, or group members may feel moved to pray a sentence prayer or repeat a verse from Scripture. It is difficult to say how long this should last, but probably just a few unhurried minutes would suffice. To round off the experience, a group member can say, 'X' (naming the person), 'the peace of the Lord Jesus be with you.'

6. *Agape feast*. Often a group will want to express their fellowship in a sharing of the Lord's Supper. If

there is no member of the group ordained to the Word and Sacrament, then within established church circles it is correct procedure to invite an ordained minister to share this with the group. Some groups, however, find it more meaningful to have an 'agape feast' instead. Again there are many ways of doing this. *agape* is one of the words used in the Greek New Testament for Christian love (see *I Corinthians* 13). So an 'agape feast' is a celebration to express Christian love. Bread and wine can be passed round the group in silence followed by a prayer or hymn of praise and thanks. Other groups choose food and drink which they feel more truly expresses their normal sharing together. As the food and drinks are passed, members can communicate, either verbally or non-verbally, what has meaning for them at that point: perhaps a word of love or encouragement to the person next to them; perhaps a handclasp or a hug to express their affection and feeling of one-ness.

THINK IT THROUGH

If touch is beginning to be part of a group's way of relating lovingly to each other, it is good to take some time in the group to talk this through.

Some people may well have fears to be allayed, and others will have questions they want answered to help them adjust to this new way of being with their fellow Christians.

It may be relevant to go over matters like:

*   What do I mean when I hug you in this group?

*   Is holding hands at the benediction not a bit of a distraction from what is happening?

*   So far, so good—but couldn't this all get a bit out of hand?

*   What would other folk think if they saw us doing this?

*   Is it really alright for ordinary Christians to lay hands on each other when they are praying for strength and healing? Is that not the task of a minister, or of a person who has a special gift from God for healing?

Remember that touch is one of the most basic of all human needs. Remember that there may be people in your group who do not have this need met for them outside the group. Remember that there may be some who do not want to be touched—and love them by respecting that, and so make it possible for them to change their minds if they choose to do so.

One of the best ways of tackling this is to have a look at the gospels of Luke and John to discover how Jesus and those around him used touch. Perhaps one or two from the group would do some research on behalf of the others, as a lead into discussion and sharing on this subject.

SPECIAL TIMES

When special seasons come—Christmas, Easter, Pentecost—or when a relevant theme is to be explored—conflict, peace, suffering—each member of the group can be invited the previous week to bring something with him to the meeting: a symbol, a poem, a meditation, a painting, a song, a record, an experience, a newspaper cutting, a bible passage, a prayer, to share with the others. During the meeting each person can share whenever he feels his contribution fits in.

TO EXPRESS EXPERIENCE

Whether or not people in your group are used to praying spontaneously it is sometimes the most natural thing in the world for one member to say, 'I really feel we ought to thank God right now for what has just happened' or, at a time when a very different atmosphere prevails in the group, 'Can we be quiet together, and then ask for God's guidance? I feel we are going round in circles!'

What matters in the worship of a small group is that it should express some dimension of the experience of the life of the group—their need for mutual forgiveness, their joy or thanksgiving, their concern and compassion.

'WHERE TWO OR THREE . . .'

When the group meets in Christ's name, he has promised to be there with you!

Part VI
PRAYER

PRAYER TOGETHER

If a group is not used to praying together except in a formal way with one person leading the prayer, then it can be quite difficult to introduce prayer of any other variety into a small group.

Many people have the idea that to pray when others can hear requires special old-fashioned language or the use of particular 'in' phrases. Merely telling people that this is not so is usually unhelpful.

Experiment with several different ways of praying in the group, especially those ways which involve everyone if possible, and those which do not require formality of any kind.

PRAYER TODAY:

A SAMPLE SESSION ON PRAYER

Many good church folk no longer pray as they were taught to at Sunday School. There are many reasons for this, some of which make sense to me. Unless your group is from a church where people still find a lot of meaning and comfort in set times of personal devotion, then many of those reasons will no doubt be aired at a session like this.

The first twelve disciples Jesus had, asked him to teach them to pray, and the prayer he gave them was very short, in spite of the fact that he himself seems to have spent hours alone with his Father.

▶ Begin the session by placing two ordinary kitchen chairs in the middle of your group. Make sure there is some space around them so they can be manoeuvred easily.

▶ Now invite the group to move the chairs into any positions that for them says something about prayer. Once the group gets the idea they will find several ways of symbolising their thoughts.

One or two examples might help—but don't give these to the group unless they need them.

'I'll put them this way. That seems like chatting to a friend.'

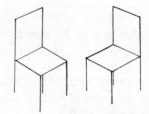

'If I place them like this, then I think how different and holy God is—we can only prostrate ourselves before him.'

'Sometimes, when I am very tired, I think I'd like God to hold me as if I were a tiny child. It's like the text, "Underneath are the everlasting arms".'

▶ When this sharing is finished and discussed, invite one or two group members to read aloud some verses on prayer, such as

> *Matthew* 6: 7 and 8
> *Matthew* 7: 9-11
> *Romans* 8: 26-28.

▶ Ask for thoughts and reactions to these verses.

▶ Give time now for people to share any experiences they wish to when prayer has been special for them.

▶ If it has not yet been shared, invite people to say what they find difficult about prayer.

▶ Move on to a time of sharing of what makes sense to the group nowadays concerning prayer, and in particular to what place prayer should have in the life of the group.

Note: This is one area where it may be impossible to come to a concensus of opinion in a small group. Do not press for a concensus. Aim for honesty and for acceptance of other people's preferred ways of praying however different they might be from that of others.

WRITING PRAYERS

Sentence Prayers

▶ If the people in your group are unaccustomed to praying aloud, it can help to give out pens and paper and suggest that each writes just one sentence of what he or she would like to say to God right now.

▶ You may suggest that it is a prayer for guidance, of thanks, of confession, a prayer for somebody else, a prayer of help for a personal situation, or whatever is right for that time.

▶ When everyone is finished writing, have the prayers either passed round the room for everyone else to read, or someone else read out aloud.
    This particular method helps those who are shy about public praying, or who cannot listen to what any other person prays in case they forget what it is they have decided to say when their turn comes.

Dialogue Prayer

▶ Suggest at one session that each person imagines that Jesus is sitting right in front of him or her.

▶ Allow a few minutes for people to decide what they would like to talk to him about if they could see him there.

▶   Now suggest that they begin to have a conversation with him and that they should write it down as a dialogue—not only what they say to Jesus, but what they imagine Jesus might reply to them.
    Give at least ten minutes for this writing.

▶   At the end of that time, suggest that folk might like to share something of what they have written, if they choose to do so.

This particular method can be varied by giving some suggestions as to what the dialogue might be about. *For instance*:

– Think about something you know you will have to do in the near future that you really don't want to do.

– Think through some situation that is concerning you just now and you want some guidance on it.

– Talk to Jesus about a relationship you have with someone which you would like to be more loving.

– Talk to Jesus about a recent incident where things seemed to go wrong, and you would like to know what you can do about it now.

– Talk with Jesus about someone you love.

After writing, suggest sharing, but give people the right to choose to opt out.

Dialogue Prayer: (a sample)

Me: Jesus, do you have a minute? There's something I'd like to talk over with you.

Jesus: Of course, Jean. What is it?

Me: Well, it's really about my friend. These past few days he hasn't seemed like himself, somehow.

Jesus: Can you tell me what you mean by that?

Me: He's normally so smiley and chatty, and he has seemed quite quiet and sort of withdrawn, somehow . . .

Jesus: And what have you done about it, then?

Me: Done, well, nothing really . . . I've just worried about him.

Jesus: And has that helped?

Me: Hm . . . I think I see what you're getting at . . . Well, no, it never does help, does it?

Jesus: What are you going to do then, that might help?

Me: You know, I think I've been thinking I was doing something because at least I was concerned enough to worry! Let me see . . . what could I do . . . I suppose I could always ask him tomorrow if there is something bothering him . . . after all, at the moment it's only in my mind!

Jesus: You know, Jean—you're beginning to get somewhere at last.

USING YOUR BODY TO HELP YOU TO PRAY

In everyday conversation each person talks, not only with his or her voice, but also talks non-verbally: with facial expressions, particular body postures and arm movements to back up what is being said.

If there is not co-ordination between what the voice says and what the rest of the body says, the person who is hearing the words and watching the body is aware of it—sometimes even at the subconscious level. Sometimes one may actually notice and remark to a friend, 'He sounded so friendly, but his smile didn't reach his eyes. They were cold.' Or you hear someone say, 'But I'm *not* angry!' and you notice he has his hands clenched. Other times, you feel uneasy . . . something is not right . . . it feels phoney, but somehow you can't pin it down.

Of course, it is possible to pray anywhere, at anytime, in any bodily position, but what you do with your body as you pray normally says something about how you are feeling inside.

▶   In your group, experiment with this idea:

Think of as many body positions you can remember that people use when they pray, and have everyone move into each of these, one after the other. After each position, share how it felt, and what it might be saying about attitudes to God, and to others.

Do not forget the more unusual ones like David dancing before the Lord (*2 Samuel* 6: 14), nor the more inconvenient ones like lying full length, face downwards on the floor!

Remember, too, that you are exploring, not only body positions for personal prayer, but also for prayer in small groups.

Some possible body postures for prayer.

Part VII
MEDITATION

MEDITATION

In formal church worship we tend to act as if silence must be avoided at all costs.

In total contrast, many of today's young people are trying out forms of meditation from the eastern religions and seem to be gaining much from them.

Medical science claims that many illnesses which appear to have physical causes, as well as those which require treatment of a psychiatric nature, are brought on, or worsened by, the pace and the stress of modern living.

Quiet meditation for a few minutes when the body is really relaxed can be as beneficial for both body and spirit as an hour's sleep—in fact, it can reach a deeper level, and do more good, physically and psychologically.

It is time that the Christian church began to rediscover the value of being quiet and relaxed in the presence of God. The great mystics of the past have done this by withdrawing to a place where they could be on their own, but there is a special dimension to the depth of fellowship in a small group when the members can meditate together. Even if there is no sharing of the thoughts and feelings that come during such a time, there is the sharing of being 'in the Spirit' together.

For many it is much easier to be silent in the presence of God when the discipline is being shared, and the time structured by someone allocated to do it, than it is to do so on one's own. If you are on your own, your thoughts often stray to 'I really ought to be doing . . .' If you are with a group, the group somehow gives you permission to spend time like this. You don't actually say to yourself, 'It must be alright, because everyone else is doing it', but it is as if you do.

In this book I will not attempt to give instructions or suggestions for the kind of meditation small groups can have together with deep relaxation, because I hope later to write a whole book on it.

In the average Sunday worship service, the scriptures are read at a pace just a bit slower than a television newscaster would read them. There is no time to think as the reading proceeds, though a phrase may strike you especially and cause you to withdraw from listening to the rest to ponder over that particular point.

If it is a story which is being read then the average mind can cope with it at a normal pace. If it is a passage from any other part of the Bible—for instance a psalm, or a deeply theological argument from one of Paul's epistles—then the average mind just cannot take it in at that speed. Either you 'hear' it, and retain nothing at all, as each new thought literally wipes out the preceding one in your mind, or you hang on to one thought which seems to be particularly relevant and challenging, and pass over the rest.

I believe that this book, which we claim as the Word of God, deserves better treatment.

The suggestions which follow can be used easily in any group wishing to be quiet together in God's presence. They require no special expertise or training.

Suggestion:

Before you commence meditating together, it will be best to check out with all the members how each one feels about silence in the group. If some members might be embarrassed by it, then discuss it further, giving the reasons why you would like to try it out. If possible, obtain their permission to try it first with a very short and simple passage, with only short periods of actual silence. After the experience, discuss how people did feel, as opposed to how they imagined they would feel.

If some are still feeling awkward, it is possibly because they have not thought how to use the silence. If that is the case, some sharing by those who felt its benefit might give the others some idea of how to tackle it more creatively the next time round.

Do not have silences longer than most members can comfortably cope with. This can be more of a strain than a refreshment.

Silence is, however, something people can learn to use and enjoy once they grow accustomed to it, and gradually lose their fear of it.

PSALM 23

One of the most familiar and best loved of all the psalms is Psalm 23. It will be best if everyone in the group has the psalm in the same translation. If you have the possibility of having it duplicated for each member, so much the better. If the copies can be marked with pen or pencil, this will be very helpful.

How to divide it for the meditation:

▶ First ask if there is anyone who would rather not read aloud.

▶ Count the number remaining, and divide the passage amongst them, in the order in which they are sitting round the room.

▶ There are six verses in this psalm, so if six people wish to read, give one verse each.

▶ If there are more, then look at the verses which easily can be understood if read with a pause between the punctuation marks, and give some members half a verse to read. (For instance, verses 3 and 4 both have two sentences each, which can be given to different people; verses 1, 5 and 6 easily divide in the middle, and still make sense.)

▶ Invite each reader to underline the part he has been allocated, as in the illustration.

During the meditation

The task of each reader is to judge how much time

the group requires to meditate on the phrase read just before his own, and to read his phrase slowly and clearly after he has given the group the right amount of silence.

It takes practice to be able to do this and to relax sufficiently before your turn to take part in the meditation, but it does become much easier, and is very rewarding.

Example

Here is Psalm 23 in *The Good News Bible* translation (quoted with permission):

1. The Lord is my shepherd;
   I have everything I need. (*Peter*)

2. He lets me rest in fields of green grass
   and leads me to quiet pools of fresh water. (*Susan*)

3. He gives me new strength. (*Margaret*)
   He guides me in the right paths,
           as he has promised. (*My part*)

4. Even if I go through the deepest darkness,
   I will not be afraid, Lord,
           for you are with me. (*Bob*)
   Your shepherd's rod and staff protect me. (*Iain*)

5. You prepare a banquet for me,
           where all my enemies can see me; (*Sandy*)
   you welcome me as an honoured guest
           and fill my cup to the brim. (*Fiona*)

6. I know that your goodness and love
              will be with me all my life; (*Sheila*)
    and your house will be my home
              as long as I live. (*John*)

WHEN SHOULD SUCH PASSAGES BE USED?

If such a meditation is taken at the beginning of a session, it sets a particular tone for the session, whether or not the passage is then dealt with in any other way—for example, by discussion or study.

If it is taken at the end of a meeting, it can provide a good rounding off if the passage chosen fits in with what has already been the subject of the session.

If a passage is being used for deeper study, then sometimes have it read in this way, rather than in a more straightforward way at a normal reading pace. Something different will be gained.

Or it can be taken as an end in itself, as completely self-contained, with no further comments necessary. Apart from the other ways already mentioned, this method can be used with any passage, and afterwards a time of sharing might take place around questions like these:

*   Which verse or phrase of what we have read do you remember best? And why?

*   Did any part puzzle you, and you would like to ask what others made of it? If so, which?

*   Did any part have a new significance for you that you would like to share with the group?

*   Was there any challenge to your feelings, your thoughts, your beliefs, your behaviour?

*   Which part would you like to pick out as something to remember especially for the next few days? Why?

SUGGESTED PASSAGES

Here are some passages in the Bible that would be good for a group to try reading in this way:

Psalm 8. 'O Lord, our Lord, your greatness is seen in all the world . . .'

Psalm 139:1-18. 'Lord, you have examined me and you know me' (this one could be tried in three sections, used at different times: 1-6; 7-12; 13-18).

Psalm 148. 'Praise the Lord!
Praise the Lord from heaven, you that live in the heights above.'

Isaiah 40:1-11. 'Comfort my people,' says our God. 'Comfort them!'

Matthew 5:3-12. The Beatitudes.

Luke 1:46-55. The Magnificat.

Romans 8:31-39. 'In view of all this, what can we say? If God is for us, who can be against us?'

I Corinthians 13:1-14:1. 'I may be able to speak the languages of men, and even of angels, but if I have no love . . .'

Philippians 2:1-11. 'Your life in Christ makes you strong, and his love comforts you . . .'

Relevation 21:1-7. 'Then I saw a new heaven and a new earth.'

Revelation 22:1-5. 'The angel also showed me the river of the water of life, sparkling like crystal, and coming from the throne of God and of the Lamb . . .'

USING ONE VERSE ONLY

The suggestion has already been made earlier that a group could begin with a shared five minutes of relaxed silence, ending with a short prayer or a verse from the Bible.

In this time, people will think their own thoughts and gather themselves together, leaving behind the stresses of life they have been involved in just prior to the session.

Another way to do this is to guide what people might think about during their five minutes or so of meditation. For example, it is possible to find many stimulating thoughts from all sorts of writers, but if you are requiring that people think about something you read to them, without their having seen it, it must be a very short sentence or phrase, or it will not be remembered sufficiently well to be meditated upon.

Many find that, as the words of the Bible are part of their common culture, a verse which is already known to them can most easily lead them into a time of silence and meditation. (Sometimes ministers will do this at the beginning of a church service, but will almost immediately erase the verse from the congregation's minds by going at once into a spoken prayer, or suggesting that a hymn be sung.)

▶ Let the leader for the session tell the group how he is planning to lead the meditation.

▶ They should then be asked to relax as much as possible, but to make sure that they are well supported as they are sitting. If the support for the body is not there, the need to shift to a more comfortable position during the silence will be uppermost in people's minds instead of the text.

▶ After that, the leader should read the verse slowly and clearly, then leave the group in silence for the time agreed upon—whether two, three or five minutes. At the end of that period he or she should read the text again, leave a short pause, and finish with an 'Amen'.

Here are some verses which might helpfully be used like this, but of course there is no limit to the variety which can be found:

> Fling wide the gates, open the ancient doors, and the great king will come in. (*Psalm* 24: 9)

> The Lord is my light and my salvation . . . Teach me, Lord, what you want me to do. (*Psalm* 27: 1, 11)

> As a deer longs for a stream of cool water, so I long for you, O God. (*Psalm* 42: 1)

> God is our shelter and strength, always ready to help in times of trouble. (*Psalm* 46: 1)

> Create a pure heart in me, O God, and put a new and loyal spirit in me. (*Psalm* 51: 10)

> When my bones were being formed, carefully put together in my mother's womb, when I was growing there in secret, you knew that I was there—you saw me before I was born. (*Psalm* 139: 15).

Those who trust in the Lord for help will find their strength renewed. They will rise on wings like eagles; they will run and not get weary; they will walk and not grow weak. (*Isaiah* 40: 31)

Any of the 'I am . . .' sayings of Jesus, which are found in John's Gospel.

Fill your minds with those things that are good and that deserve praise: things that are true, noble, right, pure, lovely, and honourable. (*Philippians* 4: 8)

Look at the birds flying around: they do not sow seeds, gather a harvest and put it in barns; yet your father in heaven takes care of them! Aren't you worth much more than birds? (*Matthew* 6: 26)

Be concerned above everything else with the kingdom of God, and with what he requires of you, and he will provide you with all these other things. (*Matthew* 6: 33)

Don't worry about anything, but in all your prayers ask God for what you need, always asking him with a thankful heart. (*Philippians* 4: 6)

A SPECIAL MEDITATION OF CONFESSION AND FORGIVENESS

If a session has included any kind of confession, openly or without actually sharing what has been silently confessed, a meditation on some verses which centre around it might be good.

The various verses could be shared amongst members of the group, or all read by one.

Psalm 130: 1-5

From the depths of my despair I call to you, Lord.
(*pause*)
Hear my cry, O Lord;
listen to my call for help!
(*pause*)
If you kept a record of our sins,
who could escape being condemned?
(*pause*)
But you forgive us,
so that we should stand in awe of you.
(*Have a longer pause here than between the other verses*)
I wait eagerly for the Lord's help,
and in his word I trust.
(*Another longer pause*)

I John 1: 8-9

If we say we have no sin we deceive ourselves and there is no truth in us . . . But if we confess our sins to God, he will keep his promise and do what is right: he will forgive us our sins, and purify us from all our wrongdoing.

USING A FEW SCATTERED VERSES ON A THEME

If your group is an ongoing one, it will possibly meet at times of the year which have particular significance for Christians. Whether or not the theme chosen for that session fits in with the time of the Christian year you may wish to use, say, a three-verse meditation at the beginning or the end of the meeting to provide time for thinking about its significance together.

It is quite effective to choose three phrases or verses and have them read with a three minute silence after each. That takes about ten minutes.

Here are some suggestions:

Christmas:

This very day in David's town your Saviour was born—Christ the Lord. (*Luke* 2: 11)

Immanuel—God is with us. (*Matthew* 1: 23)

Glory to God in the highest heaven,
and peace on earth to those with whom he is pleased. (*Luke* 2: 14)

Holy Week:

My Father, if it is possible, take this cup of suffering from me! Yet not what I want, but what you want. (*Matthew* 26: 39)

Save yourself if you are God's Son!
Come on down from the cross! (*Matthew* 27: 40)

My God, my God, why did you abandon me? (*Matthew* 27: 46.)

Easter:

The doors were locked, but Jesus came and stood among them and said, 'Peace be with you.' (*John* 20: 26)

Jesus said to Simon, 'Do you love me?' 'Yes, Lord,' he answered,' you know that I love you.' Jesus said to him, 'Take care of my sheep.' (*John* 21: 16)

I will be with you always. (*Matthew* 28:20)

Pentecost:

This is what I will do in the last days, God says:
I will pour out my Spirit on everyone. (*Acts* 2: 17)

and then, with pauses between each of the gifts, read:

The Spirit produces love . . . joy . . . peace . . . patience . . . kindness . . . goodness . . . faithfulness . . . humility . . . and self-control. (*Galatians* 5: 22, 23)

Part VIII
SYMBOLS

THE USE OF SYMBOLS IN WORSHIP

When Jesus talked with people he used the everyday things of life to communicate truth in a memorable way. He talked about salt and yeast, pearls and houses, sowing seed and mending clothes.

To stimulate groups to share thoughts and discover meanings it is possible to use his technique of talking about or pointing to the everyday things of life.

Once a group is introduced to this use of symbols, the members will be able to contribute creatively when a new symbol is passed round, or placed in the centre of the group for this purpose.

One way of introducing this is to use the ones with which they will be familiar, for example the ones used in Scripture: light, salt, bread, and so on.

To start the group off, introduce the symbol and ask members to share the thoughts triggered off by it. Verses of scripture or short prayers on the theme can then be shared as worship.

A LIT CANDLE

One that is very effective to begin with, is the symbol of light. It seems to have a significance for everyone.

If you wish to use this, dim or switch off all electric lights in the room. In the centre of the group place a candle in a simple holder. Strike a match, and light the candle.

After a moment or two spent in silence, invite the group to share any thoughts stimulated by watching the candle flame.

Examples of such sharing might be:

— Jesus said, 'I am the Light of the World.'

— He also said, 'You are the light of the world', didn't he?

— That was when he said that he wanted people to see the kind of good things we did as his followers.

— When I see that flame flickering it fills me with joy—the kind of joy that's beautiful while it lasts—like candles on a child's birthday cake.

— I can feel the heat beginning to come from the flame. It's a symbol to me of the warmth of the fellowship I've been experiencing here.

— Somehow, the flame is so gentle and soft that we all look relaxed and lovely—the way God's children ought to be!

After such sharing, and the restful pauses between sharings, the leader might finish off by praying in words that reflect the essence of what others have shared.

Alternatively, the leader might have previously chosen a short passage from the Bible which talks about light. One that would be conducive to further worship would be a few verses from the end of the Bible.

– John had a vision of the city of God, and he wrote in *Revelation* 21: 23, 24:

> The city has no need of the sun or the moon to shine on it, because the glory of God shines on it, and the Lamb is its lamp. The peoples of the world will walk by its light, and the kings of the earth will bring their wealth into it.

or

– In his first letter, John wrote to his fellow Christians:

> Now the message that we have heard from his Son and announce is this: God is light, and there is no darkness at all in him. If then, we say that we have fellowship with him, yet at the same time live in the darkness, we are lying, both in our words and in our actions. But if we live in the light—just as he is in the light—then we have fellowship with one another, and the blood of Jesus, his Son, purifies us from every sin. (*1 John* 1: 5-7)

The leader might feel that the group had already supplied enough words, and might simply suggest that hands are linked round the group while there is a minute or two of silence.

OTHER SYMBOLS WHICH CAN BE USED IN THIS WAY

After a group has used this technique on a few occasions the members will be able to think up their own symbols, but I will suggest a few more which might be helpful, or might provide stimulation for your own thoughts:

A rosebud, an opening rose and a falling rose.

A bare winter twig with buds.

A flower bulb.

A glass of water.

A piece of electrical equipment with no plug attached.

A treasure box, unopened.

An interesting looking rock or a few contrasting pebbles from a beach.

A blank sheet of paper or an unexposed film.

A teddy bear.

A cushion.

A puppet.

An old comfortable pair of shoes.

A picture made in the group of the outline of every person's hand with a crayon. (To do this, have a large sheet of paper on the floor. Hand the crayon to one member who will then invite another member to lay his hand on the paper while she traces the outline around it. She will then hand the crayon on to another person, and the process is repeated till everyone's hand has been traced on the paper. Some will overlap others and so on, which will provide food for thought later.)

A box of liquorice allsorts, or a jar of assorted sweets.

A wedding ring.

A jigsaw.

Have another session with a candle, but this time, light it and blow it out again two or three times in silence. Light it again, and then let it burn while members relate their thoughts.

If your group members enjoy using symbols for sharing, have a complete session where every person is asked to bring along a symbol of something he or she has been thinking or feeling since last the group met. At the session, use the symbols, presented one at a time to the group, to listen to each other and to grow to love and understand each other more fully than before.

BANNERS

As your group comes to have its own identity, certain times together, or events, or symbols used in the group will come to have a special significance for you.

If this happens, you might enjoy creating a banner about whatever has come to be special.

In Europe we have a fine history in our churches of beautiful stained glass windows. These windows often depict scenes from the Bible, and have a text written on them. They are usually in memory of some person or event connected with the church in which they have been installed. Few churches nowadays want to afford the tremendous cost of stained glass, but the people of God still want to express their faith through art forms. Banner making can be a good and inexpensive way to do this.

First of all, there would have to be some idea about what the banner should proclaim.

Next, the group, or someone with a special flair for design in the group, should make a simple sketch containing a symbol and some words which convey the message.

When this is agreed upon materials can be purchased or produced from rag-bags.

The banner can be any size that suits the location where it will be hung. If it is to be in a home, then it could be up to a metre in length, or only half that size.

Hessian or felt are suitable materials for the banner's background. The shapes for the words and

Some simple banners.

symbols can be made from scrap material; fine material if they are to overlap, thicker and perhaps self-coloured if they are to stand out boldly against the backcloth.

If some people in the group enjoy sewing, then the shapes can be sewn to the backing, if not glue them in place. Glueing is much quicker and can be done a bit more easily as part of a group's activity at a single meeting.

If your parish has a network of groups, then on some occasion when the various groups come together, banners made by the different groups could be hung around the church hall, and used to communicate to the other groups something of what is happening elsewhere.

A piece of dowelling threaded through the top and the bottom of the banner will make it easy to hang.

Part IX
DRAMA

DRAMA

In the middle ages only the wealthy had the privilege of being given any formal education, so the ordinary people could not read. Printing was not invented, and even if folk had been able to read, they could not have afforded a hand-written copy of a gospel. Under these conditions the church began to use drama to communicate simple Bible stories to the people in the market place.

Then came a time when acting was regarded as sinful by many Christian people, and so its common use was dropped by the churches.

Nowadays, however, drama is slowly being accepted back into the life of the church. Many congregations at least have some kind of dramatic presentation of the Christmas story by the children in the Sunday School.

One of the many ways of bringing a familiar story freshly to life is by straightforward dramatisation. In a small group it is possible to have no audience, but to achieve total group participation. This means that no-one need feel unnecessarily embarrassed or left out, which ever way you look at it.

Here is a simple guide to follow, should your group choose to try this for itself.

▶ Choose which story will be acted.

▶ Have it read in the group.

▶ Ask for volunteers, or assign parts. Make sure everybody knows which part is his or hers.

▶ Have a moment or two of quiet while each person thinks through how to act the part chosen.

▶ Set any simple scenery which is necessary or helpful—do not overdo it!

▶ Act out the story, either using the words in a modern translation, or, better still, have people use the words they would have used had they been present when the drama first took place.

▶ Sometimes it is helpful to have someone as the narrator, and read the Bible passage in between the speaking parts, but it can make the acting stilted.

▶ When the acting is finished, have a moment or two of quiet while the impact of what has been shared is felt.

▶ Ask each person in turn, 'How did you feel in the role of X?' 'Did anything come home to you in a new way?'

▶ Finally, ask if what has been experienced in the group has any relevance for the group members' lives today, and if so, what are they going to do about it?

A FEW SUGGESTIONS

1. *The Christmas story.* Acting this in a house group with adults takes away all comments like 'Oh, isn't she sweet as an angel!' and, 'Look, one of the wise men is wiping his nose on his sleeve!'

Adults have quite a different reaction to young children to a birth having to take place in a stable, for instance.

Give everyone parts—which might mean that some will have to be cattle or sheep.

There are very few words recorded as having been said in this story as it is written in *Matthew* 2:1-11 and *Luke* 2:1-20 so the group will have to decide whether to mime or invent words.

If the main part of the group meeting's time is to be spent in dramatisation in the Christmas meeting, for instance, then include also some acting out of the story where the angel tells Mary she will give birth to a son (*Luke* 1: 26-38). After that, go on to the stories in *Luke* 2 of the journey to Bethlehem, the birth in the stable and the visit of the shepherds. The *Matthew* story of the visit of the wise men takes place some time later, and so should be acted last.

If, on the other hand, the acting is only to be an introduction to the theme for the meeting, it would be best to choose just one of these main parts to the whole story to dramatise.

2. *The story of Zacchaeus.* This is found in *Luke* 19: 1-10. You won't need a tree; a kitchen chair will do admirably. Tell the crowd to give the greedy chief tax-

collector a bad time, and not to spare their comments when he casts his dignity to the winds and climbs the tree. Feel what the folk might have felt then.

3. *The healing miracles.* These are most effective to dramatise. You might like to try one of the following:

Blind Bartimaeus: *Mark* 10: 46-52.

The ten lepers: *Luke* 17: 11-19. (You will not need ten.)

The man with the demons: *Luke* 8: 26-39

The paralysed man with four friends: *Luke* 5: 17-26.

(It is not necessary to make a hole in the ceiling to act this out, but try to make is as realistic as possible!)

The main thing to achieve when the healing miracles are being dramatised is to try to get inside the skin of the person who is needing healing, and then experience the healing.

Although this part can only be taken by one person (with the exception of the ten lepers' story) it is salutory to suggest that the group spend one or two minutes with their eyes closed, trying to get in touch with how it would feel to be that person, before and after the healing.

*   *   *

An example of how dramatisation might be woven into a group session is found on pp. 127-31 of this book, entitled 'The Use of Possessions'.

*   *   *

Have a reason for choosing to dramatise a story in preference to merely reading it in a group.

For example, one of the healing miracles suggested above, the man with the demons, might well help some people in the group to feel quite frightened if it is acted well—just as the people felt who were there in the original scene.

If the topic for the meeting is, say, mental illness and how the group can support those going through it, or their relatives, then just because many people are afraid of mental illness through lack of understanding, it would be an excellent introduction to the sharing and discussion.

The ten lepers' story could be used to bring to the feeling level a session on folk others shun today.

Part X
EVALUATION

WHAT IS GOING ON? IS THIS WHAT WE WANT?

It is difficult to say exactly when a group should take time to evaluate its life. I believe it should be done at least twice a year. If, however, interest seems to be flagging, or the group is not operating according to the ideals it shared at the beginning, it is time to stop, and think through what is happening.

If evaluation is done by asking the various members how they feel about the group at that moment, this will not provide any accurate help in changing anything that ought to be changed. It may give a clue to the fact that some changes are desirable.

I will outline a particular programme I made up to try to find out why there was discontentment in a particular group, and what could be done about it. It may be that you could use the ideas by adapting them to your particular situation. I judged that there were three main areas in which this group were not pulling together:

1) how the group should be led and by whom

2) the purpose in their meeting together

3) the content of the meeting—what should be done together to achieve their purpose.

A SAMPLE EVALUATION MEETING

All the group members knew they were coming to an evaluation meeting.

First, I handed round sheets of paper I had cut out in the shape of an egg. (I got that idea from a book and thought it was quite corny, but just because it was a gimmick, I thought a point might be made!)

I then explained that eggs were meant to hatch, and new life come forth, and invited all my fellow-members to write on their egg-shaped paper a prayer for the night's meeting. When we had all written something I suggested that (a) we would believe that God would answer the prayers and (b) we each take on the responsibility for our own prayer-hatching!

We then passed round all the 'eggs' so that everyone was aware of the prayers of the others.

The filling out of the evaluation forms came next, followed by us again passing them round so that everyone could see what everyone else had chosen. We followed this by open discussion, and finished with a time of silence together and the benediction.

The following meeting collations of all the evaluations were handed round, and again they were discussed before we went on to that evening's agenda.

EVALUATION FORMS

1: PURPOSE:

The aims of such a meeting should be:

a)

b)

c)

d)

2: LEADERSHIP:

Please tick the one you think is best for you in this group.

It suits me best if:

a) a chosen leader leads it each time, and that person decides what will happen at every group meeting

b) a chosen leader leads it, but asks for suggestions from the group members as to the content of future meetings

c) a chosen leader is in over-all leadership, but the members are invited occasionally, and only if they wish to, to lead the group for one session

d) a chosen leader is in over-all leadership, but all the members share the responsibility of leading the group in their turn

e) there is no chosen leader, but all members operate in the group as they feel they ought or want to each meeting, with no set agenda

f) there is no chosen leader, but all members operate in the group as they wish to each meeting, the agenda for a series of meetings having been previously agreed on by the members

g) (Write your own choice of style if this is different from those above.)

3: CONTENT:

Please put a tick in one of the right hand columns for each activity. You are voting on whether any particular activity mentioned should be on the group's agenda

a = always, u = usually, s = sometimes
o = occasionally, n = never.

	a	u	s	o	n
a) prayer					
b) Bible study					
c) sharing of thoughts and opinions on matters of common interest in discussion					
d) sharing of current personal joys or problems for support and understanding					
e) silence					
f) guided meditation					
g) singing or listening to music					
h) reading from books other than the Bible					
i) working together on a common project					
j) instruction in the Christian faith					
k) sharing the Lord's Supper					
l) celebrations (happy times together to mark special occasions)					
m) 'exercises' to stimulate thinking and sharing					
n) speakers on specific subjects					
o) visitors (to join in whatever is happening)					
p) planned outside visits——recreational					
——educational					
q)					
r)					

210

4: PLUS AND MINUS

One very simple and effective method of doing an informal evaluation was passed on to me recently.

On a large sheet of paper, draw a line dividing the space in two. One one side draw a plus sign, and on the other a minus. Invite the group members to write on the paper in the plus area the things they have been enjoying in the group, and on the minus side, what has been worrying or disapointing them about the group in the past few meetings.

The sheet of paper is then passed round, or displayed where all can see it, to provide a basis for a discussion, decisions about change, and a celebration.

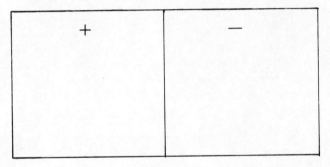

EVALUATION THROUGH BIBLE STUDY

Since the very basis of our fellowship is in the New Testament, it makes sense to use it to ask ourselves if we are carrying out its advice in the way we are operating as a group. Here are a few possible passages to use for evaluation sessions. Each one has a slightly different emphasis from the others, so could be used at different times as the group life evolves.

ONE BODY, BUT DIFFERENT PARTS
HAVING DIFFERENT GIFTS

▶ Read together *Romans* 12: 4-8.

Background:
This is not the only passage where Paul likens the Christian community to the body of Christ, but it is a compact, and easily understood one. In it he refers specifically to gifts that are not always those which people think of as important, but which are gifts that are vital to the life of a Christian group.

To share and discuss:

*   In this group, do we work together as the different parts of a body do? If so, then discuss how you see this happening; give examples.

*   Think of each group member in turn. Take time to reflect on each person, how their varying gifts are being felt and seen by the rest of the group. For ideas, look first at the list of gifts in the passage, but remember there are other gifts not mentioned there that could be part of your group's gifts for each other.

Examples:
'Dorothy. You are one of the kind ones mentioned in verse 8. Do you remember that time when Tommy had measles and I had a visitor staying with me? It was you who took her into your home for a week during that time . . . and you did it cheerfully, just as Paul says you ought to!'

'Gordon. I think your particular ministry is one of listening. I always feel that you are understanding and supporting me if I share something with you, although you are pretty quiet and do not say much.'

* Are there any of the gifts Paul mentions in these verses that seem to be missing from our group? If so, do we need them? If we do, what should we do about it?

Background information:
The method used in this study and the next is named FEEDBACK. A person does not normally know what another person feels and thinks about him. This knowledge is often assumed, but rarely checked out. In a loving group a great deal of very positive reinforcement towards new growth can come about if there is opportunity provided for such feedback. There are several ways of doing this, and here are a few suggestions chosen out of many. None of the feedback exercises are very profitable unless there is plenty of material available to feed back. In other words, unless the members of a group have come to know each other so they have things they want to say to each other, this cannot be done effectively.

> Note: To be any use, feedback must be authentic. Don't say what you don't feel. Feedback should be positive. People already know lots of negative things about themselves, and this is not the time to lengthen that list.

214

'SPEAKING THE TRUTH IN A SPIRIT OF LOVE'

Note: For some obscure reason this phrase is often used to justify a Christian's passing on, in a very negative way, something he or she feels another 'really ought to know for his own good.' The truth can as easily be something kind and lovely to encourage another, but it is surprising how few folk come under conviction that something positive 'ought to be' passed on.

▶ Have *Ephesians* 4: 15, 16, 25-32 duplicated for the group in such a way that the scripture passage is on the top half of a sheet only, leaving the rest blank to be used in the session. Have enough copies made so that each person has one for every other person in the group. (If your group has ten members, then duplicate one hundred copies.)

▶ Make sure everyone has something to write with, then hand out the sheets.

▶ Ask each person to go through the sheets given to him or her, writing the name of each other person in the group at the top of one of the sheets. (Margaret will then have a sheet marked 'Billy', one marked 'Sandy', one marked 'Mary', and so on.)

▶ Now read the passage, and spend some time sharing with each other around questions like:

* Are we growing and building up the body of Christ in love by what we say to each other in this group?

* Have we ever shared openly in this group when we were angry with one another? If not, why not?

* Are we forgiving to each other, or have we nothing to forgive?

▶ Now, in a spirit of love, invite each group member to write on the sheets before him or her, something for each other group member. Remind them that what they write has to be in keeping with the spirit of the passage in Ephesians.

▶ When all the writing is over (allow roughly 4-5 minutes for each person in the group) distribute to each member the sheets marked with his or her name.

▶ Spend a time reading these silently, then allow some time for people to respond to what others have written to them in any way they wish. Make certain that everyone clears up anything he or she does not understand completely which has been written on their sheets. If you don't you might get some misunderstanding or resentment where positive feedback was intended!

BEING AND DOING

▶ Read together *Romans* 12: 9-21.

▶ Ask each person to go over the passage by himself, thinking of incidents in the life of the group where some of the things mentioned in the passage happened.

▶ Now have a time of sharing where each person contributes what he or she has thought about.

▶ Look now at the verses which mention things that have not been happening in your group, and discuss:

*   Is this because there has been no opportunity for these to happen?

    or

*   Is our group not functioning as Paul suggests a Christian community should?

*   What should we do, if anything, about the conclusions we have reached on the above questions?

LOVING

Read through *I Corinthians* 13 and the first
sentence of 14: 1.

Share and discuss:

* Apart from love, which are the wonderful gifts that
Paul writes of in verses 1-3?
   The way your group functions, are you valuing any
of these more than love?

▶ Ask the group to read silently verses 4-7.

▶ Now invite each to underline the one phrase about
   love in that passage he feels he most lacks, but
   would like to have.

   Example: 'Love never gives up; and its faith,
   hope and patience never fail.' (Verse 7 in *Good
   News*)

▶ Now share around the group which phrase it is
   you underlined.

▶ Have a short time of prayer, with each person
   laying his hand on the shoulder of the person on
   his right, and praying for her to receive the gift of
   loving in the way she has just shared.

▶ After that, as a stimulus to help answer the prayers, ask each person to write down one simple step he plans to take to help him to answer his prayer the next time he is in a situation where he might do an un-loving thing.

▶ As a group, read again from verse 8 to the end.

▶ Invite each person to think, and then to share, what it is she most looks forward to knowing on that day when our knowledge will be complete.

Share and discuss:

* If you had that knowledge now, would it help you to be a more loving person?

In John's gospel, 13: 35, Jesus said, 'If you have love for one another, then everyone will know that you are my disciples.'

* Are outsiders to your group able to see that you are loving one another, and linking this to the fact that you are Jesus' disciples?

* Do outsiders experience any loving from your group members as a result of all the loving you receive in your group?

Part XI
CONCLUSION

There is a search today for new ways of being the Body of Christ in the world.

Two thousand years ago, people remarked, 'See how these Christians love one another!' There is an obvious discrepancy between that supportive fellowship and our current practice of burdening 'the willing horse' to breaking point and expecting his personal faith to bear him up. Good church folk need to be loved too!

Without love, life is meaningless. The crises of human experience—and special efforts by local congregations—still bring people hopeful of finding acceptance there, back to the church. If love is not offered and experienced, why should they stay?

One of the many ways forward for the church is through the formation at the local level of networks of caring groups. Hopefully, this book has provided a launching pad for some congregations to take a leap of faith into this experience.

BOOKS WITH MATERIAL FOR USE IN SMALL GROUPS

Expressing His Life. Celebration Publishing. Lytchett Minster, Dorset.

A very intensive course of Bible study related to deepening christian community. Each participant is expected to do an hour's preparatory study before each group meeting and bring resulting thoughts as a basis for sharing. Material for six courses each of four meetings. Leaders' Pack includes two handbooks for leaders, a study manual for participants and a cassette of four short talks.

Serendipity—a mini course on Christian Community. Lyman Coleman.

All India Catholic University Federation,
1/16A Sterling Road, Madras 600 034.

An excellent, easily adaptable series of over 50 sessions designed to enable a small group to grow into being a Christ-encountering community. Especially suitable for younger folk. (This is edited from a more expensive and comprehensive series of books published by Word, Incorporated, U.S.A.)

Study on the Community of Women and Men in the Church.
World Council of Churches
P.O. Box 66, 150 route de Ferney
1211 Geneva 20, Switzerland.

An exciting modern group study guide aimed at helping church men and women to think through the challenges involved in new styles of partnership and community for the church in today's world.

The Secret of Staying in Love. John Powell. Argus Communications.

A book designed primarily for two person relationship enhancing, but one which has several ideas which can be adapted for use in small sharing groups.

Values Clarification. Simon, Howe and Kirschenbaum. Hart, U.S.A.

A book full of exercises to enable groups to think through their beliefs and value systems in a stimulating and challenging way.

Awareness. John O. Stevens.

Full of suggestions for deepening awareness for individuals, couples and groups.

Work With the Word. Ephesians. Philippians. British and Foreign Bible Society.

This is a new series of aids for individual and group Bible Study. The workbooks are designed to help individuals do preparatory study as a basis for sharing at the group study. Good for groups who want to get to grips with the content of the epistles.

Born to Win. James and Jongeward. Addison Wesley.

A most helpful book for groups to learn about interpersonal relationships through a study of transactional analysis. At the end of each chapter is a series of suggestions for individual and group involvement and exploration.

Born to Love. Muriel James. Addison Wesley.

This is a book written primarily for the American church, vividly portraying the life of a typical congregation, and explaining what is going on through transactional analysis. At the end of each chapter there are experiential exercises for individual and group participation.

OTHER BOOKS WHICH MAY BE OF HELP

Berne, Eric. *Games People Play*. Penguin, 1970.
Lewis, C.S. *A Grief Observed*. Faber, 1961.
Morrice, J.K.W. *Crisis Intervention—Studies in Community Care*. Pergamon, 1976.
Snyder, Ross. *Inscape*. Abingdon, 1968.
Westberg, Granger E. *Good Grief*. Fortress Press, 1962.

I give you a new commandment: Love one another;
as I have loved you, so you are to love one another. If
there is this love among you, then all will know that
you are my disciples.

John 13:34,35.

It is love, then, that you should strive for.

I Cor. 14:1.